THE SURPRISING GOSPEL

THE SURPRISING GOSPEL

Intriguing Psychological Insights
from the New Testament

WILHELM H. WUELLNER
and
ROBERT C. LESLIE

Abingdon Press
Nashville

THE SURPRISING GOSPEL

Library of Congress Cataloging in Publication Data

WUELLNER, WILHELM H., 1927–
   The surprising gospel.
   Bibliography: p.
   Includes index.
   1. Bible. N.T.—Psychology. I. Leslie, Robert C.
(Robert Campbell), 1917– . II. Title.
   BS2545.P9W84 1984   225.6   83-21413

ISBN 0-687-40724-9

Scripture quotations in this publication unless otherwise noted are from
the Revised Standard Version of the Bible, copyrighted 1946, 1952, ©
1971, 1973 by the Division of Christian Education of the National Council
of the Churches of Christ in the U.S.A., and are used by permission.

Excerpts from AFTER THE FALL by Arthur Miller. Copyright © 1964 by
Arthur Miller. Reprinted by permission of Viking Penguin, Inc. and
International Creative Management, Inc.

MANUFACTURED BY THE PARTHENON PRESS AT
NASHVILLE, TENNESSEE, UNITED STATES OF AMERICA

To Flora and Paula

CONTENTS

PREFACE

TO READ THE NEW Testament with an interest in psychology is to be constantly surprised. In an amazing way the New Testament faith deals with the depth dimension of life, with the deeper dynamics that come into play in almost every human interaction. To ferret out some of these dynamic forces and demonstrate how the New Testament deals with them is the primary purpose of this book. Illustrations are drawn from contemporary literature in several cultures to highlight the issues.

The book is a joint enterprise. It represents the collaborative efforts of a New Testament scholar, Wilhelm Wuellner, and a psychological practitioner, Robert C. Leslie. When New Testament exegesis is informed by a psychology that has both depth and height, and when psychological insights are challenged by a spiritual orientation that takes theological thinking seriously, a powerful combination results. Our intent is to deal responsibly with the biblical text and, at the same time, to help the Christian message become alive for every day.

The biases of the authors will be quite readily apparent. Wilhelm Wuellner takes exception to many of the traditional approaches to the New Testament and develops an approach that sees a dynamic relationship between elements of the texts and that invites a personal response to the biblical ideas. Robert C. Leslie draws on several strands of psychological theory but makes heaviest use of the attitudinal values of Viktor E. Frankl, the symbolic approach of C. G. Jung, the interpersonal theory of Harry Stack Sullivan, and the family systems approach of Virginia Satir. All four of these writers stress an ego-psychology approach in which persons are seen as taking active roles in deciding how their lives will be lived.

Both Wuellner and Leslie are currently exploring the impact of culture on their respective disciplines, and an interest in intercultural and cross-cultural concerns will become apparent. The Bible is seen as a document growing out of its own Palestinian culture—a culture very different from our own. To highlight these differences is to become more aware of how many differences are present whenever people come together out of whatever cultural backgrounds.

The intent of the authors is to stress the need for inclusive language. We are very conscious of how male-oriented both the biblical record and much psychological thinking really are. We have chosen, however, to retain the language of direct quotations, whether from biblical or secular sources, reminding the reader that only in quite recent times has a sensitivity to inclusive language developed. Moreover, the inclusive language issue reminds us how considerably biblical language differs from psychological language.

One organizing principle which we have used in selecting the order for the passages considered is the lectionary. As is indicated at the beginning of the notes for each chapter, the passages start with Advent, move through Epiphany, Lent, and Pentecost and conclude with All Saints' Day. The message of the text is related to the Christian community and to the choice made to hear certain messages at particular times of the year. Thus the texts are significant not only for counselors, but for preachers and Christian educators as well.

Incentive for developing this material comes from a class taught jointly at Pacific School of Religion several times in the last few years. The many ideas in this book are indexed to provide focal points of interest for students of scripture, psychology, and literature.

CHAPTER ONE / WAITING

THE NEW TESTAMENT begins with an enigma. Something inexplicable has occurred: a child is conceived without a biological father.[1] And all involved wait, not knowing what to expect.

In seven short verses Matthew introduces Jesus as Christ, the son of David and the son of Abraham. If our Western, scientific, fact-oriented mind is offended by the story of a virgin becoming pregnant without the help of a man, then Matthew has achieved his purpose. He wants to bring us up short. He wants to signal that something very surprising, something very much out of the ordinary *has* taken place, and, in our reading, *is* taking place.

The very first sentence in the first chapter of Matthew sets the stage. Jesus is presented as the Messiah of the Old Testament, yet as Christ, the anointed one in an entirely new sense.[2] "The book of the genealogy of Jesus Christ" (Matt. 1:1) is a new kind of genealogy, a new beginning, a rebirth.[3] And the genealogy is itself an enigma, for the descent of Jesus is given through Joseph, but Jesus is not the biological son of Joseph. He is "the child of the Holy Spirit" (1:19).[4]

Matthew's intent is further revealed in the names of the four women who appear in the genealogy: Tamar, who committed incest (Gen. 38:6ff); Rahab, a harlot (Josh. 2:1ff); Ruth, a foreigner (Ruth 1:4ff); and Bathsheba (i.e., "the wife of Uriah"), an adulteress (II Sam. 11:2ff). It is not by chance that Matthew introduces these four women.[5]

13

He wants to make it clear that even the scandals of incest or harlotry or adultery, ordinarily thought of as stumbling blocks, can become the occasion for growth.[6] It is as if he is alerting his reader in the first chapter: "Be prepared to think in unusual, paradoxical ways."

Matthew invites us in the dramatic story of 1:18-28 to read the gospel in a dynamic sense. Marjorie Casebier McCoy, theologian and actress, sees the birth narrative as a theological statement:

> The "virgin birth," or more accurately the virginal concep-
> tion, of Jesus is mentioned only in the infancy stories in the
> Gospels of Luke and Matthew. Their vivid artistry points to
> the meaning of Jesus as the Messiah, Son of God, making
> them Christological reflections rather than historical
> descriptions.[7]

If the story is meant to be history, it is history as symbolic of a process that goes on within any person's life, a process in which inner and outer, facts and meanings, real and unreal merge into a harmonic unity. Novelist Mary Ellen Chase in *Windswept* writes in this same mode. She describes the feelings of John Marston as a boy when he sat in the chapel high on a promontory at Windswept on the coast of Maine:

> From the beginning of his devotion to the place there had
> been mingled with his love of it a kind of pleasurable awe,
> from which in later years . . . he never entirely freed him-
> self, an undefined, yet recognized, sense, on the one hand,
> of the homeliness and naturalness of sacred places and
> objects, and, on the other, of the spiritual counterparts
> of those things which are to most children, and, indeed,
> to most persons . . . , the merely familiar. Here within the
> walls of the chapel outward and inward things met, merged,
> were woven together, lost their separation one from the
> other.[8]

There are three special aspects of Matthew's advent story that we want to deal with. All three accent waiting.[9]

Being sensitive to life's deepest meanings

The first is the sensitivity of Joseph to life's deepest meanings. Matthew's account of the birth of Jesus is Joseph's story, just as Luke's account (see chapter 2) is Mary's story. Joseph discovered that his fiancée, with whom he had not had sexual intercourse, was pregnant.[10] It is not difficult to imagine the mixed emotions that such a situation would evoke. Both Joseph and Mary found themselves in a dilemma. Because Joseph was a "just man" and was "unwilling" to put Mary to "shame," he put aside his feelings of anger and hurt pride and "resolved" to deal with her "quietly"[11] (1:19). He was willing to wait.

Up to this point the story is not an uncommon one. It demonstrates how people are caught up in social systems, where one person's behavior calls forth another person's action. The betrothal relationship in Judean Jewish culture prescribes which patterns are acceptable and which ones are not. The "just" Joseph reacts in the only way that a "shame" culture[12] permits him to act. To avoid public shame, Joseph "resolves" to dissolve the betrothal contract "quietly" (i.e., privately). Then Joseph has a dream.[13]

The key to understanding Joseph is recognizing his capacity to be in touch with the deeper parts of his own life. Marjorie Casebier McCoy sees Joseph as "open to hearing the deeper voices within himself and willing to affirm his visionary dream of God's presence in his relationship to Mary."[14] The same power at work in Mary's womb is now also at work in Joseph's unconscious in a dream[15] (see also 2:12).

It is not only Joseph who is called upon to listen to an inner voice. Mary Ellen Chase writes of the impact of a young, stern New England headmaster on the boys who attended his academy. Phillip Marston had been at the academy only one year, but he

> knew that its headmaster had unrelenting hold upon
> some Reality which no boy could understand and which

15

few men would ever experience, save perhaps in fleeting glimpses. . . . [The headmaster] still exacted, and expected, from his boys their best and from most of them got it, because in failing him they were uneasily conscious of failing some greater demand than his own.[16]

The problem is that it is all too easy to allow quick anger over hurt pride to dictate behavior so that deeper meanings are never pursued and the inner voice is crowded out. Psychiatrist Fritz Kunkel describes the struggle that people in Joseph's situation experience:

Joseph is confronted with the dark forces of his own nature; hurt pride fights against love, and anger struggles with self-control. Joseph, and that means everybody in such a decisive moment, has to face himself. He has to face destiny. The weird power which has cornered him is greater than he is.[17]

Viktor Frankl is a psychiatrist who acknowledges a power that is greater than himself. When, as a Jewish doctor in Vienna shortly after Hitler had taken over Austria, he was offered a chance to escape Nazi tyranny by migrating to the United States, he responded in a typical fashion. He said that to leave Vienna would mean leaving his elderly parents to their certain death. Before he could make such a decision he would need a "hint from heaven."

Should I really leave them, simply saying goodbye? Or should I rather stay with them at the risk of following them into a concentration camp? When pondering these thoughts again and again, I found that this was the type of situation in which one would need to get a hint from Heaven. Then I went home, and as I arrived there I noticed a piece of marble stone lying on a table. "What is that?" I asked my old father, and he reported that he had found it on the site where the largest Viennese Synagogue had stood until the day when the National Socialists destroyed it by burning it down. "And why did you take it with you?" I replied. "Because it is a piece of the two tables containing the Ten Commandments." In fact, it showed a Hebrew letter engraved and engoldened. And then my old father added, "I can even tell you which commandment it signifies. This letter is only to be found in the abbreviation of one of the Ten Commandments." "And which one is it?" I inquired eagerly and curiously. And the answer was, "Honor father and mother, and you will dwell in the land." So I stayed with father and mother in our country—and definitely declined at the same moment to pick up the visa.[18]

Recognizing God's presence in history

Kunkel's reference to "the weird power" leads to our second emphasis: "God with us" (1:23*b*). Matthew's reference to the fulfillment of prophecy with the quotation from Isaiah 7:14 (1:22-23) is only one of many such references. Indeed, a distinctive aspect of Matthew's writing is his deliberate intent to demonstrate how the present is related to the past. The fulfillment of Old Testament prophecy is indicated in this passage and in many others as well.[19] Moreover, the transformation of Mary's life, now affecting Joseph's life as "son of David," then Israel, and finally "all nations" (28:19), is of divine origin and destiny. The origin concerns Jesus as "son of David, son of Abraham" (1:1). In the three lists of fourteen generations each (Abraham to David, David to Exile, Exile to Jesus), Jesus appears in the last list as the thirteenth of fourteen, thus pointing to "his people" (1:21) as the destined goal.[20]

In bringing in the fulfillment of prophesy, Matthew is asserting the presence of God in history. *Emmanuel* means "God with us" (1:23).[21] No matter what the calamity is, God is there with us.[22] In Mary Ellen Chase's *Windswept*, the solemn note of death is introduced early in the story when Phillip Marston, who built Windswept, is killed in a hunting accident by a shot from a rifle in the hands of his son's chum. Jan, the handyman and devoted friend, asks young John, the bereaved son, to read a prayer from the *Book of Common Prayer* at the grave.

> "It is not easy for you, . . . but it has come and we must do as your father said. We must not leave him here without a prayer to God. I cannot read the words straight and right,

17

and there is no man here who knows this book. You must read them yourself. You will be glad some day that you did. My own book says it is, what you say, Advent Sunday, the time of the Lord's coming to this earth. . . ."

Then they all stood together by the open grave, and John Marston read the words that Jan had marked in his book.

It was the collect for Advent Sunday. In all the years afterward that they read it in the chapel at Windswept, . . . its prayer for grace to cast away the works of darkness and put upon us all the armour of light now in the time of this mortal life, they were to see that little group of men standing about John Marston on that vast brown summit of land beneath that whitening sky.[23]

It is clear that Mary Ellen Chase believes that the armor of light is sufficient to penetrate the powers of darkness. In Matthew's Gospel the powers of darkness are dramatically represented by Herod (2:1-18), among others. The massacre of the children ordered by Herod, the king who administered Judea in the name of Rome, points to the realistic presence of the power of evil always ready to oppose the forces of good.[24]

One of the reasons that Viktor Frankl speaks so powerfully to many people today is that he experienced the awful evil of the concentration camp but persisted in making something good come out of it. When he was first taken to a concentration camp, he lost the manuscript, written in shorthand, for the book which was eventually published as *The Doctor and the Soul.* Believing with all of his being that a person's life is determined not by what life brings but by the response that is made, he demonstrated how meaning could be found even in the terrible circumstances of the camp. He cites his own reaction to the loss of his manuscript, confiscated on his arrival at Auschwitz:

I had to surrender my clothes and in turn inherited the wornout rags of an inmate who had been sent to the gas chamber immediately after his arrival at the Auschwitz railway station. Instead of the many pages of my manuscript, I found in the pocket of the newly acquired coat a single page torn out of a Hebrew prayer book, which contained the main Jewish prayer, *Shema Yisrael.* How should I have interpreted such a "coincidence" other than as a challenge to *live* my thoughts instead of merely putting them on paper?[25]

When Frankl talks of the challenge to live out his ideas, he is speaking like a religious person. He writes: "The religious man experiences his existence not only as a concrete task but as a personal mission which is given to him by a personal Being. Thus he sees his task transparently, namely, in the light of Transcendence; he alone can in spite of all say 'yes' to life under all conditions and circumstances—in spite of all; in spite of distress and death."[26]

To live under God ("in the light of Transcendence") does not mean that the powers of darkness will go away, but it does mean that the light is seen more clearly in the darkness. Kunkel reminds us how necessary it is to face the darkness: "Matthew shows us at every intermediate step in every chapter and almost in every verse that the way down is the way up, that facing darkness may mean the discovery of light, that death can become life."[27]

Being open to change

Our third emphasis is on the action that resulted from Joseph's dream. Joseph's earlier "resolve" (1:19) gets transformed so that "he did as the angel commanded him" (literally "orderly outlined for him," 1:24). Instead of dissolving the engagement, "he took his wife" (commits himself to marriage, 1:24) without having sexual intercourse with her ("knew her not," 1:25) until Jesus was born. Then, in obedience to the angel's instruction (1:21), he, the son of David and Abraham, designated the new creation as Jesus (Joshua).[28]

To hear the inner voice (the angel) calls for a willingness to change, to be transformed. To be transformed is to respond to the dream. Arthur Miller, in his play *After the*

Fall, describes the dilemma faced by Quentin, a middle-aged lawyer, who walks into a courtroom, his usual, familiar place of working. But when he looks toward the bench where the judge usually sits, he finds that the bench is empty.[29] No one is there to make definitive judgments. He is driven back to his own resources. Later in the play, Holga, whom Quentin hopes to marry, talks about the necessity of taking responsible action, of making necessary change: "I think one must finally take one's life in one's arms, Quentin."[30]

Psychiatrist M. Scott Peck speaks of the willingness to change and to be transformed as an obligation "to be God":

> To experience one's closeness to God is also to experience the obligation to be God, to be the agent of His power and love. The call to grace is a call to a life of effortful caring, . . . of service and whatever sacrifice seems required. It is a call out of spiritual childhood into adulthood, . . . to be a parent unto mankind.[31]

Joseph was called upon to be a bigger man than his initial anger and hurt suggested. Dr. Peck notes that often psychiatric problems develop when people accept promotion to positions of higher power and greater responsibility. To avoid such problems, some people prefer not to be promoted, to simply coast, allowing personal feelings to dictate behavior, choosing the line of least resistance.

It was not only Joseph who was called on to change. In a culture that emphasizes shame, the whole family matrix is involved. The embarrassment of Joseph could not be healed without involving his extended family and Mary's family as well. The change called for was much more than an individual matter.

It is commonplace to find people leaving psychological treatment when it becomes apparent that mental health means taking a responsible stand. But it is also true that growing into greater maturity brings with it a remarkable sense of freedom. Dr. Peck notes that progress in psychotherapy often results in changes in persons from a sense of powerlessness in the presence of overwhelming circumstances to a realization that "they have it in their power to do whatever they want."[32]

What Dr. Peck expresses in psychological terms has been expressed even more dramatically in biblical words. Lives that are lined up with God's power find a new source of strength for action, and this strength is found in waiting:

> . . . They who wait for the Lord
>   shall renew their strength,
> they shall mount up with wings
>   like eagles,
> they shall run and not be weary,
>   they shall walk and not faint. (Isaiah 40:31)

Chapter Two / Glorifying

[LUKE 2:1-20]

LUKE'S ACCOUNT OF THE birth of Jesus is Mary's story, just as Matthew's account is Joseph's story. By placing a young mother with a newborn infant in center stage, Luke activates a response that touches the human heart in a way that Matthew's "shrill discord"[1] never does. The unforgettable imagery of shepherds watching over their flocks, of angels singing in the fields, and of a crowded inn with a manger crib for an expectant mother touches a deep, responsive note in even the most calloused person.

The surprising element in the story is the unexpected way in which the birth of the Messiah is presented. Here is no king—only a tiny baby. Here is no throne—only a crude stable. Here is no capital—only a little town.[2] Here are no distinguished guests—only seemingly simple shepherds glorifying God.

A second look at the shepherds, however, adds an even more surprising note. According to the first-century Jewish historian Flavius Josephus, the shepherds were reputed to be "revolutionaries" or "zealots."[3] As is so often the case when deeper reflection challenges first impressions, the "simple" shepherds turn out to be not so simple, and their presence in the story of the birth of Jesus adds a jarring note to the idyllic scene.

Most surprising of all is the central place given to Mary. Whereas the biblical record is written largely in masculine terms, here is a story in which a woman plays the more dominant role. The Swiss psychiatrist C. G. Jung has devoted a good deal of his writing to pointing out how much the Western world has ignored the dimension of the feminine and by doing so has largely ignored a major aspect of life. Pastoral psychologist Ann Belford Ulanov, whose writing is based on Jungian thought, points out that as long as the feminine element is de-emphasized, "the fulness of human experience is not represented."[4]

A woman chaplain who spent a summer working for the Seamen's Institute in New York and New Jersey tells how important the feminine principle was in her work. She found that the eyes and the voices of seamen on the docks were asking her:

> Is there indeed something in this place that we can believe in? Is there anything powerful here, besides the power of the dollar and the machine, the steady decay of industry? Be the angel for us, be the white-robed Master's daughter, the fearless woman who takes away our fear.

She goes on to say: "And it was terrifying, sometimes, to find that by simply appearing there, I had in some way become that woman—the Master's daughter, the good mother, the beloved, the trusted sister, Joan of Arc."[5] Her presence added a dimension of immeasurable importance to their lives.

It is not difficult to understand why Mary has been given such a central place in Christendom. She is the person, McCoy notes, "around whom Christians regroup their experience of the feminine in the life of faith, a way to offset the excessive masculine dominance in the Christian church."[6] Moreover, it is not the first time that a major religion has honored a virgin mother. The Egyptian mother-goddess Isis "was worshipped as a virgin mother and as lady of sorrows and intercession."[7] The point is that God in Christ is a part of the human process in a way that calls for an act of faith. How better to present the faith dimension than to suddenly confront a logical, rational, scientific world view with a virgin birth!

In this passage there are four elements we wish to lift up.

Stressing the power of God

The first is the polarity of earthly powers versus the power of God. Our life, that is, the life of the "people on earth," is shaped by two forces, two systems. On the one hand are the earthly conventions or powers. These may be Caesar's political forces, Caesar's cultural and social control, or the regional or provincial extension of it in the legate Quirinius. They may also be the competing cultural traditions of Judaism, David's house and city (2:4, 11) yearning for fulfillment through liberation. And they may be the innkeepers in our life, providing the dwelling places for our existence during life's journey.

On the other hand there is God. Several times Luke refers to God "in the highest" (2:14). Jesus will be called "the Son of the Most High" (1:32). The angel, speaking to Mary, told her how "the power of the Most High" would overshadow her (1:35). Zechariah's prophecy noted how the child would be called "the prophet of the Most High" (1:76).[8]

The religious life involves a constant tension between the claims of secular forces and the claims of God. Kierkegaard, the Danish Christian philosopher, entitled one of his books *Either/Or*,[9] thus stating in unequivocal language the choice set before every person devoted to God. *Either* God is given first place in a person's life, *or* the relentless demands of secular interests take over. Jesus was very clear in stating priorities: "You shall love the Lord your God with all your heart, and with all your soul, and with all your mind, and with all your strength."[10] In Jesus' temptations, in which he laid down guidelines for his own life, he declined each of the devil's tempting offers in favor of holding steadily to a God-directed life: "You shall worship the Lord your God, and him only shall you serve" (Luke 4:8).

It is the therapeutic world that reminds us, however, that to separate the conflicting claims of lower versus higher powers is often not easy. Psychiatrist M. Scott Peck describes one case in which the "higher" powers in a young woman's life so controlled her that she became what he called "the most frightened person" he had seen.[11] For this patient, whose name was Kathy, the need was to grow out of a rigid, perfectionist kind of religion in which God was perceived only as a punishing tyrant. Then Dr. Peck describes another patient, Marcia, in whose life the need was to rediscover a positive place for God in her life. He tells of the two different directions that therapy took: "Through therapy Kathy moved from a place where the notion of God was all-important to a place where it was of no importance. Marcia, on the other hand, moved from a position where she rejected the notion of God to one where it was becoming quite meaningful for her."[12]

The question the Christmas story asks is: Whom will we please, God in the highest, or other forces in life? The message of the angels to the shepherds accented this polarity. An awareness of "God in the highest" (2:14) is related to peace among people on earth. Only among God-pleasing people will there be peace. We, the people (therapy-seekers and therapy-providers), will have no part in Christmas if we fail to "please God."[13]

Nurturing divine action

The second issue in this passage is the contrast between the way in which the divine action is nurtured and the way it is opposed. The new life as promised gets delivered, tended, and nurtured in an imaginative, idyllic scene (2:5–7a), but the first of many obstacles is also encountered when there is no room in the inn (2:7b).

Nurturing has long been considered a feminine attribute, but Ann Belford Ulanov reminds us of how the nurturing aspect is only part of the feminine picture:

> Next to the figures of the good nurturing mother is the dark figure of the witch. Next to the image of the Madonna with the newborn Christ-child suckling at her breast is the image—placed in our liturgical calendar only three days after Christmas—of all those other mothers crying without consolation because of the Slaughter of the Innocents.[14]

The slaughter of the innocents in Matthew's Gospel is represented in Luke's Gospel by the fact that there was no room in the inn. We might note, parenthetically, that a quiet, warm manger may have been a better place for a birth than the noisy, crowded, common room of the inn of that day. L. Paul Trudinger reminds us how easy it is to read into this story our own modern Western customs: "This was no modern hotel, or even 18th Century English inn. . . . There would most probably be just one large room where everyone stayed. Here they all bedded down, dressed, and washed if the luxury of water were available. At a busy time, such as during a census, the room would be packed."[15]

Whatever the circumstances may have been, to be confronted by a No Vacancy sign is always a blow. The incident is a reminder that opposition is a normal part of life. There is no such thing as an absence of pressure. The title of a book, made into a popular song, is very true: *I Never Promised You a Rose Garden.*

The Swiss psychiatrist C. G. Jung writes about neurosis as *unlived suffering.*[16] By this term he is suggesting that obstacles are a very normal part of life and that attempts at avoiding them lead to neurosis. Roy Fairchild, an able interpreter of Jung, puts it in these words:

> Neurosis can be understood as the suffering of a human being who has not yet discovered what life means for him. A person's symptoms (e.g., depression, apathy, anxiety, and compulsive activity) alert the individual that it is time to move on to the next step in his development. He finds that next step . . . in becoming aware of the unlived life in him and in identifying where it is trying to move.[17]

As we will see throughout this book, Jung sees the problems of contemporary persons as growing out of efforts at avoiding the pain of growth. He sees religion as integral to the psychological journey as his oft-quoted statement asserts: "Among all my patients in the second half of life—that is to say, over thirty-five—there has not been one

27

whose problem in the last resort was not that of finding a religious outlook on life."[18]

Responding with fear and joy

The third issue centers in how the new life in God affects our life. The prospect of new life generates both fear and joy. It generates fear[19] because it intersects with our life at times when we are preoccupied with doing our duties in the fold, watching over the flocks, guarding our charge against "evil." Although the negative overtones of fear are most commonly recognized, there are positive aspects to fear, too. It is fear of failure that often prompts action from an otherwise placid and satisfied stance. It is realistic fear that prompts caution and concern for those who need guidance and protection.

The new life in God also generates joy.[20] The joy comes because of the prospect of deep-seated, long-harbored dreams and hopes for ourselves and our world. The new life in God is life as it is meant to be: eager, full of hope, childlike. Arthur Miller has a line in which he describes this mood. Quentin, the middle-aged lawyer, is speaking: "Every morning when I awake, I'm full of hope! With everything I know—I open my eyes, I'm like a boy! For an instant there is some—unformed promise in the air. I jump out of bed, I shave, I can't wait to finish breakfast."[21] Quentin goes on to describe the accompanying fear: "—and then it seeps in my room, my life and its pointlessness. And I thought—if I could corner that hope, find what it consists of and either kill it for a lie, or really make it mine . . ."[22]

The therapeutic task can be described as seeking to "corner that hope." Dr. M. Scott Peck notes that many persons "are routinely terrified by mental health."[23] He tells of a young woman who had gradually learned to handle a family that had tried "to manipulate her into fulfilling their unrealistic demands," which had previously left her deeply depressed. When she reported that she "felt good about it," and went on to say that she would like to "feel that way more often," Dr. Peck said that she could stay on top of things, but it would take a lot of hard work. Her response was: "I didn't come here for my life to be made more difficult. I want to be able to just relax and enjoy myself. You expect me to be some sort of god or something."[24] Shortly afterwards she terminated treatment. She was afraid of joy! Just as fear without joy is devasting, joy without fear is irrelevant.

Telling, returning, and praising

The fourth issue points to three tasks that confront us. The first task is making known to others what was made known to us (2:17ff). The second task is to return to our familiar tasks (2:20*a*). The third task is to keep on "glorifying and praising God" for *all* that was (and will be) heard and seen (but also touched, tasted, smelled, or otherwise perceived, mentally or intuitively) in life's unexpected gifts and challenges. This is what it means to have "God with us," Emmanuel.[25]

The emphasis in this third task is on *keeping on*. Glorifying God is not just a Sunday activity; it's a daily task, a lifelong task that brings God into the picture even in the midst of the most mundane activities. John Steinbeck's novel *East of Eden* is the story of men and women who struggle to keep the glory in their lives. Steinbeck is not one to write in usual religious terms. He does not write of glorifying God, but he does write of keeping glory alive. The meaning is basically the same: there is no glory in life apart from the eternal laws of God.

> I guess a man's importance in the world can be measured by the quality and number of his glories. It is a lonely thing but it relates us to the world. . . . And this I believe: that the free, exploring mind of the individual human is the most valuable thing in the world. . . . I will fight . . . to preserve the one thing that separates us from the uncreative beasts. If the glory can be killed, we are lost.[26]

The novel closes with the young heroine, Abra, saying: "I woke up with joy this morning." Lee, the servant homemaker, sets before her *her* task, to make known to her friend Cal the meaning of glory: "He's crammed full to the top with every good thing and every bad thing. I've thought that one single person could almost with the weight of a little finger . . ."[27] and the reader knows that Abra is God's agent who can bring glory into Cal's life.

CHAPTER THREE / REFUSING

[MARK 5:1-20]

EMBEDDED IN A STRIKING story of exorcism is an unexpected surprise: Jesus' refusal to allow the man healed of a demon to accompany him. The story itself, as told in Mark 5:1-20 (with parallels in Matthew 8:28-34 and Luke 8:26-39), is a graphic one of a man "with an unclean spirit" who tortured himself and was forced to live among the tombs, "bruising himself with stones." When the unclean spirit is exorcised, the man who had been possessed with demons, now in his right mind, begs Jesus to allow him to join the disciples, but Jesus refuses the request.

To Western ears, this story is a strange one. We are not accustomed to talking either about unclean spirits or about demonic possession. But in Mark's Gospel there are ten other specific passages referring either to unclean spirits or to demons,[1] and obviously in the time of Jesus this was a common way of speaking. From the early mention in 1:23-28 of a man healed of an unclean spirit to the final affirmation in 16:17 that the disciples "will cast out demons," there is an acceptance of the presence of demons as a natural part of life.

Even today, in a country like Taiwan, demons play a major role in everyday life. The countryside abounds with village temples where the spirits are consulted in preparation for virtually every important decision. And in Chinatowns all over the world, on Chinese New Year, dragon processions accompanied by firecrackers intend to drive out evil spirits from homes and business establishments as the new year begins.

Indeed, when the man in Mark's story, who was called a demoniac, names himself Legion, he is giving apt description to a feeling experienced by many people even in our own day. "My name is Legion," he said, and then went on to explain, "for we are many." The sense of being torn apart by conflicting feelings is an easily recognized experience.

The need to become integrated, to be healed as a unified being, is commonly felt. Psychiatric literature is full of case studies of people who experience multiple personalities,[2] and even very normal persons have a sense of being invaded by alien thoughts and unwanted feelings. Anne Frank writes in her diary:

> I've already told you before that I have, as it were, a dual personality. One half embodies my exuberant cheerfulness, making fun of everything, my high-spiritedness, and above all, the way I take everything lightly. This includes not taking offense at a flirtation, a kiss, an embrace, a dirty joke. This side is usually lying in wait and pushes away the other, which is much better, deeper and purer. You must realize that no one knows Anne's better side and that's why most people find me so insufferable.[3]

There are three issues of special concern in this passage.

Finding acceptance

The first issue of interest to us in this passage is the kind of acceptance that the demoniac found in Jesus. The Reverend John Sutherland Bonnell points out how different the attitude of Jesus was as compared with that of the townspeople. "For the first time in this wretched person's life, he was face to face with one who was not afraid of him, in whose eyes he saw not the hate and fear he was accustomed to see in the eyes of other men, but compassion and understanding."[4]

Harry Stack Sullivan, a psychiatrist who had a special feel for mentally ill persons and who had a special gift for making contact with them, spoke of three aspects of a personality as the "good-me," the "bad-me," and the "not-me."[5] All of us know of the "good-me," the positive aspects of our personality which we can claim and with which we identify. We know, too, of the "bad-me," that part of our personality which we dislike and recognize as somehow undesirable. The "not-me," however, is of a different sort. It is that part of the personality which is so unacceptable that it is hidden from consciousness. It is as if the person is saying: "That is really not a part of me. That is too unacceptable to be claimed by me as a part of myself." The "not-me" is thus separated from the conscious personality. It becomes the sick part of the personality. The task of therapy is to bring back together the "good-me," the "bad-me," and the "not-me." The task calls for a therapist so obviously accepting that even the "not-me" can be recognized as acceptable.

As the story of the demoniac unfolds, we find the man transformed in the presence of Jesus. Although such transformations are rare, they do happen. Carroll Wise, the chaplain at Worcester State Hospital, tells of watching Harry Stack Sullivan effect a transformation in a mentally ill patient. Dr. Sullivan was a visitor at a regular clinical case conference where a schizophrenic patient was being presented. The doctor who was working with the patient admitted to having had no success in even making contact of any sort. In the demonstration at the case conference he tried, without success, to establish any kind of communication. Sullivan was then invited to try. Chaplain Wise reports what followed:

> Sullivan's first move was to edge his chair just a little closer to that of the patient and to lean forward so that he could look directly at the patient in a very friendly, warm manner. To the amazement of all, the patient responded to every question and comment that was made by Dr. Sullivan. For

half an hour or more they conversed together, seemingly oblivious to the fact that there was anyone else in the room.[6]

By edging closer and leaning forward, Sullivan indicated a special acceptance of the patient. It may well have been the same kind of attention that Jesus gave to the demoniac.

A vivid illustration of the power of acceptance is found in the novel by Theodore Isaac Rubin called *Lisa and David*.[7] Two young adolescents, in the treatment ward of a psychiatric institution, create for each other a climate of acceptance in which each is able to move toward health. Lisa sees herself as two persons: Lisa and Muriel. She holds her fragmented self together by always talking in rhyme. David is a brilliant but brittle boy who is controlled by the fear that the touch of another person can mean his death. When David accepts Lisa's peculiar pattern of rhyming as the terms of relating to her, and puts his own words in rhyme, and when Lisa accepts David's fear of being touched and is careful not to get too close to him, each begins to move out of illness toward health. Their acceptance of each other was not dependent on anyone's changing, but was an acceptance "in spite of" peculiar, even unreasonable behavior. In the climate of acceptance, each could risk growing toward health.

The nonacceptance of the demoniac is made clear by the details of the story. His enforced isolation from the community was complete. He lived alone among the tombs, so wild that no attempt at confining him by chains was successful. Cut off as he was from everyone, it is no wonder he was sick. The Old Testament story of Cain and Abel tells graphically of Cain's predicament when, condemned because of the murder of Abel, he is sentenced to be "a fugitive and a wanderer on the earth" (Gen. 4:12). Cain's cry of protest is the cry of anyone in any age who is isolated from his community: "My punishment is greater than I can bear" (Gen. 4:13).

Exorcising demons

When the exorcising of a demon is seen in the light of the whole of Mark's Gospel, the point of the story becomes clearer. "Jesus, Son of the Most High God" (5:7),[8] has the power to unify fragmented parts of a person, to transform a raving maniac into a self-possessed person sitting properly clothed and in his right mind.[9] The details[10] of the exorcising of the demon are unclear,[11] but the thrust of the story is clear: what was formerly unmanageable, painful, and destructive became controlled, happy, and constructive. Energy that was tearing the demoniac apart and breaking out in fearsome and threatening ways was brought under control and channeled into useful patterns.

It is ironic that the messianic secret that Jesus is the "Son of the Most High God," is affirmed by a very unlikely person, by a demoniac. One might have expected such a declaration to have been made first by one of the disciples, but instead it was made by an unknown and unnamed person who was afflicted with a serious illness. Once again the surprising nature of the gospel is accented.

Rollo May, in his book *Love and Will,* deals at some length with a discussion of what he calls the "daimonic." He sees the "daimonic" as a force that is found within every person and has tremendous power both for evil and for good. It is the creative energy with which every person is endowed which can become distorted and malignant (excessive aggression, hostility, and cruelty) or channeled and constructive (unusual creativity, concern, and altruism). It is "the urge," May writes, "in every being to affirm itself, assert itself, perpetuate and increase itself."[12] When the urge becomes thwarted, it can become aggressively destructive.

The destruction of the swine in the gospel story is a peculiar detail that might represent the release of energy which, when bound up, had resulted in illness. Symbolically, the swine that "rushed down the steep bank into the sea" (5:13) suggest the tremendous force which had been bound up in the man's illness. It is as if the potential for creativity becomes malignant when not channeled and released productively. When released from being repressed, it explodes in unexpected ways. Kunkel suggests that it is the nature of things to have some negative side effects in the redemption process:

> When redemption takes place, the negative powers turn positive. The split is replaced by wholeness. Why, then, do the demons rush into the swine and the swine into the lake? If the redemptive process would reach ideal completion, such a thing would not happen; but nothing on earth is complete. Even Jesus could not convert the Pharisees.[13]

In the story there is a movement on the part of onlookers that parallels the change in the demoniac. Starting with fear (5:15), they then begged Jesus to leave (5:17),[14] but finally "marveled" (5:20). Implications for us in our own day are obvious.

Saying no

We have stressed the importance of demonstrating acceptance in order to establish contact with persons in need. As a first step, acceptance is essential. But acceptance alone is not enough. An important book for parents carries the title, *Love Is Not Enough*.[15] The thesis of the book is that even in the demonstration of love, there are times when saying no is essential. Even though there is a natural reluctance to say no, it is quite clear that people can live with a no.[16] What people cannot live with is uncertainty or evasion or deception. James Dittes, pastoral psychologist, has written a helpful book entitled *When the People Say No*.[17] His point is that opposition, when it is recognized and worked with, often leads to a much deeper understanding of the issue. A careful reading of Mark's Gospel discloses a number of times when Jesus said no either by words or by action.[18] Central among them is the story of the demoniac.

The request of the demoniac after the demons had left him was quite natural. So grateful was he for what Jesus had

36

done for him that he asked to stay close to Jesus. But Jesus refused his request. Like any good counselor who recognizes an unhealthy dependency, Jesus sent the man back to his friends at home. To be completely integrated, to be a unified person called for more than simply becoming one of Jesus' followers. It called for an active program on the man's own part of taking the initiative. It called for going home, back to where it is likely his problems originated. And it called for telling ("began to proclaim") "how much Jesus had done for him" (5:20).

There is a vivid illustration of breaking dependence in Arthur Miller's play *After the Fall*. Felice, a dancer who had been helped through a divorce by her lawyer Quentin, puts him on a pedestal and "blesses" him every time she sees him, actually raising her hand in gesture of blessing. In the final scene of the play, Quentin interacts with each of the significant persons in his life. When he comes to Felice, she raises her hand in the peculiar gesture of "blessing." But instead of accepting her dependent relationship, Quentin reaches out to shake her hand, thus "aborting her enslavement."[19]

When Jesus refused to allow the restored man to accompany him, he was making clear that the restoration to health was more than an individual matter. The whole community of which the man was a part was involved. In true Eastern style, Jesus saw the man not as an isolated individual as Western ways might suggest, but as a part of a web of relationships in community life. Over and over again as we study the gospel record, we will find this emphasis on being in positive relationships with others.

CHAPTER FOUR / CONFRONTING

[JOHN 4:1-42]

THE CONVERSATION THAT Jesus had with the Samaritan woman at Jacob's well is full of surprises. In the first place, Jesus didn't act like the people of his day. The disciples "marveled that he was talking with a woman" (4:27).[1] Men simply didn't engage women in conversation in that day, especially at noon in a public place. Moreover, the woman was a Samaritan, and as she herself said: "Jews have no dealings with Samaritans" (4:9). And finally, the woman was of questionable morals, having had five husbands and now living with another man to whom she was not married.

It was a surprise that Jesus was in Samaria at all. The record reads, "He left Judea and departed again to Galilee. He had to pass through Samaria" (4:3-4). As a matter of fact, it was not true that he "had" to pass through Samaria. Most Jews traveling from Judea to Galilee avoided hostile Samaria[2] by detouring through Perea on the east side of the Jordan River. But Jesus was not one to avoid unpleasantness. He dealt with issues—even difficult, interpersonal ones—head on. He was a living testimony to the affirmation that facts can be faced, whatever they are.

When Jung referred to neurosis as unlived suffering,[3] he was thinking of attempts at evading the truth. We have only to consider the extremes that some families go to to avoid dealing with an illegitimate pregnancy or an abnormal child or a run-in with the law to realize how life can become complicated when efforts are made to evade the facts. Indeed, the testimony of the whole psychoanalytic tradition

39

is that facts can be faced, but attempts at evasion are disastrous.

An unexpected feature in this passage is the way Jesus turns a commonplace request for a drink of water into a therapeutic encounter. The story is written in John's typical fashion. Based on literal historical references, John develops a symbolic approach through his gospel, as is vividly illustrated in the account of the birth of Jesus (1:1-14).[4] The Samaritan woman's story, like the accounts of Nicodemus (3:1-12), the paralytic (5:1-18), and the blind man (9:1-35) starts with a specific incident, then moves into theological discourse. At the time the gospel was written, the need was to stress the theological message, "that you may believe that Jesus is the Christ, the Son of God, and that believing you may have life in his name" (20:31). A psychological equivalent of this theological statement might be, "that you may be fully integrated as a whole and unified person and so know life in all its height and depth."

There are three issues we want to deal with in this passage.

Recognizing defensiveness

The initial dialogue between Jesus and the Samaritan woman is an almost classic description of how a defensive person responds to a simple request. When Jesus asks the woman for a drink of water, her response is to ask a question challenging the appropriateness of his making any request of her—"a woman of Samaria" (4:9). Like any good counselor, Jesus recognized the defensiveness of her response and made no effort to answer her question.

It is commonplace to discover that behind most angry responses lies some personal hurt. Dr. Irene M. Josselyn tells of a difficult adolescent girl who eventually told her:

> People say that I have a terrible temper. I don't think so. Someone says something to me that hurts awfully and it makes me mad that they would hurt me, so I go off by myself and comfort myself until I get over it. Then people say I am sullen and don't care about anybody. I'm afraid to show I

care because my feelings get hurt so easily. I know it's silly, but I get mad when people hurt my feelings.[5]

I (RCL) recall working with a couple in marriage counseling where almost any topic led to a quarrel. On one occasion the dialogue went like this:

Kay: Have you made up your mind about staying in Oakland or moving to Sacramento?

Ben: *(angrily)* Well, what do you want me to say?

Kay: Don't yell at me!

Ben: I'm not yelling!

RCL: Let's stop here a minute. Ben, what did you hear Kay say to you?

Ben: I heard her criticizing me for procrastinating. She always wants me to make quick decisions. But it's too complicated for that.

RCL: *(to Kay)* Kay, what did you mean to say to Ben?

Kay: I meant to ask if we had thought through the practical questions about staying versus moving. I was amazed when he jumped at me. I just meant to open up a conversation. I didn't have any intention of talking with him about his not making decisions. Neither of us is much good at making decisions.

RCL: Let's try it again. Kay, how could you say it to give a clearer message?

It took relatively little effort to help this couple sense how easy it was to set off each other's defensiveness.

The clue to the Samaritan woman's defensiveness comes in the reference to the time of day when this dialogue is set. The reference to "the sixth hour" (4:6) needs to be understood as meaning noon. The time for women to draw water from the town well[6] is seldom at noon, in the heat of the day. The usual time would be early morning, at which occasion the women of the city would gather not only to draw water for the day but also to exchange gossip and enjoy each other's company. Jesus recognizes that finding a woman alone at the well at noon said something quite specific about her relationship with the other women. She appeared to be isolated from them.

Virginia Satir is a psychiatric social worker who has stressed the systems of interpersonal relationships in which each person is involved. Her book *Peoplemaking*[7] demonstrates how any one person can be understood only by seeing how that person relates to many others, and especially to family members. Satir would find the approach used by Jesus with the Samaritan woman congenial because Jesus was sensitive to how the woman related to her family and to her community.

It is of considerable interest that it is the woman herself who introduces a community emphasis.[8] She continues to be on the defensive, noting that Jesus has nothing to draw water with, but she adds a quite personal note when she identifies herself with her Samaritan group: "*our* father Jacob." Jesus responds to her continued defensiveness by ignoring the personal challenge ("Are you greater than our father Jacob") and by creating an imaginative image of water that quenches the deepest kind of thirst.

It is noteworthy that the refusal of Jesus to respond to her defensiveness prompts her to drop her defenses and ask for help: "Give me this water" (4:15). I (RCL) recall meeting a veteran of World War II who was militantly objecting to anyone who took a stand against the role of the United States during the Vietnam engagement. When the veteran was given a chance, in an accepting and supportive group climate, to share his life history, the reasons for his position became clear. While on the front lines as a G.I. during World War II, he had mistakenly fired upon a patrol of his own buddies who were bringing in prisoners on a dark, fog-covered night. Not receiving the password in response to his challenge, the veteran fired into the darkness, killing all of the patrol. As he told the group of the burden of guilt he had carried for so many years, the vehemence of his position on Vietnam was understandable. His attack was his own way of handling his deep inner guilt. There was a reason for his defensiveness! It was only when he felt supported rather than attacked that he was willing to reveal what he was really feeling.

Confronting discrepancies

We have noted before that Jesus was not merely accepting and supportive.[9] He did not hesitate to take a stand and to confront discrepancies, and his dialogue with the Samaritan woman bears this out. He put his finger on the immorality of her life and did not allow her to gloss over it.

It is especially instructive to note Jesus' timing. His confrontation came only after the woman had dropped her defensiveness and had asked for help in a quite personal way. It was only then, and not before, that Jesus confronted her with the facts of her life.

Virginia Satir works in this same fashion. She first of all gives her counselee the sense of being supported. Some of the support comes from the affirmation that any one person's problem is also the person's family's problem; that the problem is less an individual matter than it is a family concern. Satir points out that although a family generally "identifies" one member as being the problem member ("identified patient"), she believes the whole family is the problem. The solution is to break up the family "system," the patterns of interaction that keep unhealthy relationships operating. The method is to identify unhealthy patterns as they emerge and to confront them directly.

Unhealthy relationships often emerge, as they did in Jesus' encounter with the Samaritan woman, when something ambiguous is uncovered. Psychiatrist Paul Tournier tells of working with a woman who appeared to be much younger than she was. He reports his conversation with her as follows:

> "How old are you?" I ask her.
> "Thirty-six."
> "But you look at least ten years younger!"
> "Yes, everyone says that I look very young."
> "I wonder why that is? There must be a reason. Do you think that some person or thing has prevented you from growing up?"

There is a long silence, while the woman sits lost in thought. At last she says to me: "Do you mean my mother? She always treats me as if I were still a little girl."[10]

Tournier goes on to report how he took the initiative to help this woman become more independent. He enlisted the help of her mother in encouraging greater independence, and he persuaded her fiancé to help break the dependency on her mother by moving up the date of the proposed marriage. He thus worked not only with the woman, but with all of the significant persons within her family system. He worked very much within the framework of Satir's family therapy.

A vivid illustration of confrontation is provided by playwright Tennessee Williams in his play *Cat on a Hot Tin Roof*. Williams deliberately uses vulgarity and profanity in his play, and so turns some people off, but he does it deliberately. He wants to say that as we confront life in all its ugliness and work through whatever life brings without evasion or withdrawal, we can emerge at a new level of relatedness which has far more depth than we had known before. Pastoral theologian Reuel Howe describes the "confrontation" scene:

In this play, Brick, the son, evaded his problems with himself, his father, his wife, and his work through an excessive use of alcohol. His father, Big Daddy, in his rough, profane way, was greatly concerned about his son. Finally, in a tremendous scene between Big Daddy and Brick, the father pursued his son through every kind of evasion and rationalization in a determined effort to break through to his heart. Nothing that Brick could say to his father was sufficient to cause Big Daddy to turn away. He could easily have abandoned his sick boy and evaded the pain of what he was trying to do. Instead, he hammered at the door of Brick's life with a love that was willing to accept every rejection that his son could offer. And he did not give up. Finally, he broke through, reached his boy, and brought him back to his life with his family and his work.[11]

Of course, confrontation is not always successful. In the case of the Samaritan woman, her immediate response to

Jesus' confrontation was to try to deflect the conversation from her personal life to the safe subject of religious worship. As religious leaders can often be sidetracked by religious themes, she hoped to distract Jesus by changing the subject and thus divert attention from herself. Pastoral counselors, in particular, are often easy subjects for this particular gambit since relating everyday life to deeper religious meanings is their life's work. But Jesus does not fall into the trap. A nice intellectual discussion of whether the mountain in Samaria or the temple in Jerusalem is the proper place to carry out worship is avoided as Jesus delves further into the subject of "spirit" and "truth" (4:24) in worship. This leads, then, to John's affirmation of Jesus as Savior of the world.

Finding meaning

The third issue in this passage concerns finding meanings. The issue is pointed up by one of the many little details in the account. In the Samaritan woman's eagerness to tell others about her encounter with Jesus, she "left her water jar, and went away into the city," and spoke "to the people" (4:28). The water jar, the symbol of her isolation from the other women of the city, is left behind as she reaches out to establish a new sense of community. Her testimony reflected a significant change in her life. From a self-centered preoccupation with her own concerns, we find her at the end of the story inviting others to look up Jesus: "Come, see a man who told me all that I ever did" (4:29).

A central feature of the Samaritan woman's story is a search for greater meaning in her life. The intensity of her search is made clear in the original Greek. When she says: "Sir, give me this water, that I may not thirst, nor come here to draw" (4:15), the sense of longing might better be expressed as: "Give me this water that I need not keep coming in this dreary drudgery, day after day, to draw water in the meaningless routine of daily existence"[12] Her life was a good expression of what Viktor Frankl refers to as the "existential vacuum," a life devoid of any significant kind of meaning.[13]

Frankl calls his therapeutic approach logotherapy. He takes the Greek word *logos,* which can be translated "word," as in John's Gospel,[14] or "meaning" (among other possibilities). Logotherapy is thus "meaning-therapy" or the "therapy of meaning." Frankl asserts that|the search for meaning is so crucial in a person's life that there is no healing, in any complete sense, without finding a satisfactory answer to the quest for meaning⌡ In Frankl's own counseling approach, he makes the search for meaning central. So he would say of a person like the Samaritan woman that her central problem is the vacuum at the center of her life, and the answer to her problem is to find a much more satisfying meaning for her life.

The problem with the Samaritan woman was that she sought meaning in too narrow an area—in relationships with men. Her need was to broaden the area in which she looked for meaning, to move beyond the pursuit of pleasure to more inclusive goals.[15] Frankl's words, spoken to a young woman who wanted a rational explanation of the meaning of her daily tasks, might have been spoken to the Samaritan woman. After asserting that the meaning of one's life is found not in leisurely reflection but in commitment to the immediate concrete situation, he declared:

> Dedicate yourself to the here and now, to the given situation and the present hour, and the meaning will dawn on you. Try to be honest to yourself in pondering your vocational possibilities as well as your personal relationships. I would do injustice to you and to your freedom of choice if I took over any decisions like these. They are up to you and therefore you should keep in mind your responsibleness. Struggling for a meaning in your life, for a life task, may be the immediate task of your present life.[16]

Chapter Five / Healing

THE NEW TESTAMENT is full of surprises. It was characteristic of Jesus that he did not work in the usual ways, that he did not think in customary patterns. People were constantly surprised by the approach that he used and were constantly challenged to think and act in new ways. This was certainly true in the case of the healing of the paralytic as recorded in Matthew 9:1-8.[1]

Any careful study of the New Testament makes it clear that healing was much more of an emphasis in the ministry of Jesus than many of us have realized.[2] When John the Baptist sent his disciples to ask Jesus whether or not he was the Messiah, Jesus referred primarily to his ministry of physical healing: "Go and tell John what you hear and see: the blind receive their sight and the lame walk, lepers are cleansed and the deaf hear, and the dead are raised up, and the poor have good news preached to them" (11:4-5 and Luke 7:22).

The surprise in the story of the healing of the paralytic is that Jesus centered his attention on the forgiveness of the man's sins rather than on his paralyzed legs. Whereas everyone else was thinking of the man's physical condition, Jesus was thinking of his total being. In a mood very similar to today's emphasis on holistic health, Jesus saw the man's whole life as being involved in his physical well-being. In focusing on the forgiveness of sins, Jesus saw the paralysis of the man's legs as a functional disorder in which the problem lay not in the legs but in the whole emotional life of the man.[3]

47

A vivid illustration of a functional disorder was the case of Elizabeth Barrett, who was a complete invalid, confined to her bed, until she met Robert Browning. To the amazement of her family and especially her tyrannical father, Elizabeth Barrett rose from an invalid's bed to marry Robert Browning and begin an entirely new life, living in Italy and becoming a poet in her own right. A new love in her life was a stronger power than the inhibiting force of her autocratic father, whose will was too strong for her to combat by herself. Her illness was more an illness of the spirit than an illness of the body, but it found expression in her body.[4]

The classic story of recovery from a functional paralysis is the case of Elizabeth von Ritter, the woman whose recovery through treatment by Sigmund Freud is told graphically in Henry Denker's play *A Far Country*.[5] Completely paralyzed and confined to a wheelchair, but evidencing no physical reason for not being able to walk, this woman achieved recovery when she was helped to face emotional trauma in the background of her life which had literally made her incapable of making any move. By working through feelings that had been repressed for a long time, she regained her health. Her paralysis was primarily an emotional rather than a physical handicap, but it was expressed in an inability to move her legs.

In Arthur Miller's play *The Price*, Esther asks her husband: "Why can't you make a move?"[6] Later, she answers her own question. "No wonder you're paralyzed— you haven't believed a word you've said all these years. We've been lying away our existence all these years; down the sewer, day after day after day . . . to protect a miserable, cheap manipulator."[7] She realizes that her husband's paralyzed state, his inability to make any move, is tied in with his whole life-style. To be able to move calls for a radical change that would shake up his entire life orientation.

It is because "being paralyzed" is so common that this story of the paralytic has so much relevance for us today. And the story is all the more important because it points to the involvement not only of a single paralyzed man, but includes also his friends, his family, the scribes, and all the crowd. There are four elements in this passage which we want to stress.

Believing as a prerequisite for healing

The healing of the paralytic took place in an atmosphere of faith.[8] Matthew does not specify who the people were who carried the paralyzed man, but Jesus points to their faith as being crucial.[9]

The importance of an atmosphere of faith cannot be overstressed. Jerome Frank, in his book *Persuasion and Healing*,[10] notes how crucial the atmosphere of faith is for any healing. Referring to the healing miracles of Lourdes, he points out how the French peasant who seeks healing at Lourdes goes with the backing of his entire village so that faith in the anticipated healing is a highly significant factor. In a communal atmosphere of faith, there is a readiness for healing.[11]

Freeing for health through forgiveness

A second element in healing is the emphasis on the spirit as the healing agent for the body. Instead of dealing with the physical problem, Jesus looks to a deeper concern. Instead of seeing the paralytic as one primarily crippled in his legs, Jesus saw him as one crippled in his spirit. Before being concerned about his physical well-being, Jesus was interested in his spiritual well-being.

It is in this same sense that Jesus proclaims God's forgiveness of the paralytic's sins. In the time of Jesus, it was believed that sin and illness were related, and Jesus was a part of the culture of his day.[12] However, there is no evidence that Jesus believed that sin was the only cause of illness. It is clear that Jesus' attitude toward sin anticipates the findings of contemporary psychotherapy in noting the close connection among emotional, spiritual, and physical well-being.

One of the fascinating fields of medical study lately is the exploration of how emotional states are related to the onset of cancer. One study uncovered data demonstrating that in 95 percent of cancer cases studied, there was an unresolved loss in the period immediately prior to the onset of the illness.[13] The emotional turmoil associated with the loss (usually the death of a loved one) created a climate within the physical organism that made the organism susceptible to the growth of the cancer cells that are always present but normally stay under control.

Pastoral counselors Newman Cryer and John Vayhinger tell of the case study of a woman who was troubled with recurrent migraine headaches that made her life miserable. When she sought professional help for the headaches, it became apparent that she harbored deep resentment against her in-laws because of their intrusion into her relationship with her husband. When, in personal counseling, she reached the point where she could understand her in-laws as well-meaning even if ill-advised, and could forgive them for their unintentional interference, her migraine headaches dramatically disappeared. By forgiving her in-laws, she restored herself to health![14]

Challenging growth

It is common knowledge that some kind of challenge is needed to effect change in a person's condition. What is less well understood is that for challenge to be effective, it needs to be preceded by some indication of support. One writer defines the therapeutic task as combining the hand extended in support with the finger pointed in challenge.[15]

In dealing with the paralytic, Jesus began with words of support, with encouragement. The term *my son* is used as an endearment. Leslie Weatherhead suggests that the "my son" might be rendered as "laddie" since the Greek word means "child."[16] In these words Jesus reaches out with words that might be used within the intimacy of a family. When the "take heart" (note also 9:22 and 14:27) is added to the "my son," the impact is that of a loving parent undergirding a child in need. The words help reduce apprehension and fear and thus make a challenge more possible.

A careful reading of the New Testament records of encounters that Jesus had with individuals demonstrates how typically Jesus initiated contact with some kind of affirming support. He understood that change is difficult, that resistance to change is easily created, and that a pre-condition for change is some demonstration of acceptance. Any marriage counselor is familiar with the attitude expressed by the housewife whose husband was critical of her housekeeping. "How can I help him to understand," she pleaded, "that I cannot find the strength to pick things up until I am sure that he loves me whether I pick things up or not?"

Acceptance by itself, however, is seldom enough. A challenge is often needed to produce results. With the paralytic, the words of support are followed by a challenge in three forms. He is challenged first of all to get up and walk, to leave the passive role of helplessness and to involve himself actively in his own recovery. Lawrence LeShan expresses this attitude in the title of his book: *You Can Fight For Your Life*. Psychiatrist Viktor Frankl puts the challenge in a somewhat similar book title: *Say "Yes" to Life in Spite of Everything*.[17] Norman Cousins has written a best-selling book, *Anatomy of an Illness*,[18] in which he describes his own self-healing after he decided to call forth the natural defense mechanisms of his own body. He appeals to physicians and patients to take an active role in learning to manage the forces of both body and mind that work toward healing.

The second challenge to the paralytic is to take in hand the very crutches which up to this point had defined his life, to pick up his bed and thus demonstrate that the bed no longer controls him.

The third challenge is to face his home, the very social, religious matrix which had in part sustained and perhaps even generated the paralysis. The recognition of the involvement of the paralytic's family in his condition is at the heart of the current approach in counseling known as family therapy. One of the ablest of family counselors (or therapists) is Virginia Satir. As noted earlier, she popularized the concept of "identified patient" by noting that although one person in a family is often identified as the sick one, it is the total family that is involved in creating and continuing problems.

For example, if a boy is found stealing cars, he is likely to be considered a juvenile delinquent. But if further investigation turns up the fact that the only time he steals a car is when his parents threaten to divorce, it then becomes apparent that the problem is not so much in the boy alone as it is in the whole web of relationships in the family.

For the paralytic to be sent home is for him to relate to his family and friends in a new way.[19]

Resisting unorthodox change

Change of any kind is never easy, and change of an unexpected sort is even harder. In the story of the paralytic, "certain of the scribes"[20] objected to unorthodox change, to a change which did not fit their system. It was not that they objected to growth; they simply wanted the change expressed in growth to follow certain prescribed patterns. The "blasphemy"[21] to which the scribes objected was the challenge to their particular way of ordering life.

There is a good bit of the scribe in most of us. Whenever there is a challenge to grow in new and unexpected ways, there is resistance. Growth is hard, and anyone trying to be an agent of growth will experience resistance. The resistance expressed in this story is typical of the kind of resistance that Jesus met whenever he surprised people by not fitting into the status quo.

In the story of the paralytic, the challenge issued by Jesus is not only to the sick man and the scribes; it is also to the onlookers as well. As Matthew puts it, the crowds were "afraid."[22] They sensed that Jesus was calling for a change not just in the paralytic but in the whole social order as well. They resisted change. They did not want to be disturbed in their own way of life and so were afraid.

The kind of change Jesus was calling for had been referred to earlier in the passage known to us as the Lord's Prayer. The significant words are:

> And forgive us our debts,
> As we also have forgiven our debtors. (6:12)

Jesus was reminding the people that they could forgive people who had wronged them, and that this was God's way. "They were afraid," but they also "glorified God, who had given such authority" to them (9:8, see also 18:18).

It is Fritz Kunkel who calls our attention to the "ground-shaping innovation" of this story: "Jesus is not simply a miracle-working rabbi. . . . Does he dare to forgive sins? Is he stronger than the laws of our old religion? . . . Will he destroy all our former convictions, all tradition, all reasonable ways of life?"[23]

Kunkel goes on to point out that "skepticism and paralysis belong together," and that we simultaneously are both "the paralyzed man and the skeptic scribe."[24] The story of the paralytic is no longer just the story of an unknown man with paralyzed legs. It is our story.

CHAPTER SIX / DENYING

[MARK 14:66-72]

THERE IS NOTHING really surprising in Peter's denial of Jesus. Jesus had predicted it earlier (14:26-31), and even without the prediction it could have been anticipated. It was the nature of Peter to be extreme about everything, including his insistence about his own staying power. The surprising thing is that it was Peter who became the leader of the disciples after the death of Jesus.

This passage "fulfills" what was anticipated (predicted) in 14:26-31. This prediction, like the earlier one in 8:31-33, had been vehemently *(ekperissos)*[1] and repeatedly (imperfect tense) denounced by Peter and, indeed, by all the disciples. When Peter follows Jesus, though "at a distance" (14:54),[2] right into the courtyard of the high priest's palace, he appears to have won the first round, seemingly brave and bold.

Mark's Gospel is Peter's story.[3] The book tells how Peter first meets Jesus (1:16), how he proclaims Jesus to be the Christ (8:29), how he tests Jesus (8:32), how he denies Jesus (this passage), how he remembers Jesus and weeps (14:72). It is to Peter that the women are directed to go after the resurrection (16:7).

Still, the Gospel of Mark is not written as a history of Peter and his relationship to Jesus. Rather, it is written to make new disciples of the readers.[4] How it relates to us today is our major concern. We want to deal with three issues that impinge upon our lives.

Calling forth potential

The first issue is the transformation in Peter. How can we account for the change that took place in Peter from a vacillating, boastful, somewhat arrogant fellow to the sturdy character on whom the early church was built? How was it that Jesus saw in him something that others didn't see, and called it forth?

The late Eric Berne developed an intriguing approach in psychotherapy which he called Transactional Analysis.[5] His work achieved phenomenal success, largely because of a simple formula which he set forth. Everyone, he declared, has a fully functioning adult which can be called forth to handle life's problems in even seemingly impossible situations. The problem is that most of us tend to respond to difficulties like helpless children (calling forth the child), or we fall back on patterns learned from our parents (calling forth the parent). The more constructive response is to act appropriately in adultlike ways (calling forth the adult). Berne recognizes that calling forth an adultlike response involves a process of reeducation in which the support of the therapist is of primary importance.

The supportive role of the therapist has long been recognized as the key to therapeutic progress. Viktor Frankl quotes a remark made by Goethe as being at the heart of therapy: "If we take people as they are, we make them worse. If we treat them as if they were what they ought to be, we help them to become what they are capable of becoming."[6] Frankl routinely sees the potential in people and has been remarkably successful in calling it forth.[7]

A contemporary novel gives an illustration of helping people become what they are capable of becoming. Ken Kesey's *One Flew Over the Cuckoo's Nest* tells of McMurphy, a boisterous, fun-loving, brawling rebel who turns out, unexpectedly, to be a kind of contemporary Christ-figure. Single-handedly he calls back to health a group of chronic patients in a mental ward, and he gives his life in the process. Chief, a huge native American, tells of his reaction to

McMurphy's hand, extended in greeting: "I remember the fingers were thick and strong closing over mine, and my hand commenced to feel peculiar and went to swelling up out there on my stick of an arm, like he was transmitting his own life blood into it. It rang with blood and power."[8]

Later, when McMurphy is rallying support from the chronic patients in a revolt against the Big Nurse, he needs one more hand raised to win the vote. Chief, who is thought by the nurse to be deaf and dumb and out of contact, is confronted by McMurphy: "Chief, you're our last bet." Chief tells what happened to his hand:

> It's too late to stop it now. McMurphy did something to it that first day, put some kind of hex on it with his hand so it won't act like I order it. There's no sense in it, any fool can see; I wouldn't do it on my own. Just by the way the nurse is staring at me with her mouth empty of words I can see I'm in for trouble, but I can't stop it. McMurphy's got hidden wires hooked to it, lifting it slow just to get me out of the fog and into the open where I'm fair game. He's doing it, wires. . . . No, that's not the truth. I lifted it myself.[9]

McMurphy called forth from Chief an adultlike response.

In Mark's Gospel, one clue to how Jesus dealt with Peter is found in 14:27-31, where Peter declares that, even if all Jesus' other followers desert, he will not. According to Mark, Jesus replies, "Truly, I say to you, this very night, before the cock crows twice, you will deny me three times." Here Jesus takes a very realistic stand. It is as if he is saying to Peter: "Look, Peter, we both know you are an impetuous, well-meaning person. But let's not fool ourselves about how you'll act in a crisis. You'll not be any better, or any worse, than most people. And I love you anyway. My feeling for you isn't dependent on how you perform."

The same realistic confrontation is found in the very next passage where Peter and James and John, whom Jesus took with him to the Garden of Gethsemane, are found asleep (14:32-42). It is Peter that Jesus reproaches: "Simon, are you asleep? Could you not watch one hour? Watch and pray that you may not enter into temptation; the spirit indeed is willing, but the flesh is weak" (14:37-38). This open dealing with Peter, which was characteristic of Jesus' interaction with him, builds a strong relationship. Again it is as if Jesus were saying, "You mean well. Your intentions are the best, but you continually fail to live up to them" (14:38b).

It is significant that in this passage Jesus refers to Peter as Simon. Beginning with 3:16, where it is indicated that Jesus gave Simon the surname of Peter,[10] every reference is to Peter until we come to this story in the Garden of Gethsemane. Now, suddenly, Jesus uses the old name Simon again. The connotation is that here the weak Simon is addressed rather than the strong Peter. Just as Jesus used terms of endearment to indicate his affection, so he used other terms (or names) to indicate his displeasure.[11]

Handling defensiveness

The second issue in this passage is the denial itself, repeated three times with ever-increasing vehemence. The first denial comes at a time and place when Peter had sought and found some physical comfort in the coldest part of the night, just before dawn. In the artificial light of the warming fire, the identity of Peter gets recognized from an unsuspected source: a maid. The denial leads Peter to retreat into the dark: away from the fire, away from the palace courtyard into the fore-court (14:68), near the gateway—perhaps for an escape attempt. But there will be no escape. Another gateway is needed.

The second denial is intensified as the same maid now alerts the bystanders.[12] Peter's anxiety increases. His cloak of anonymity has been torn off. It is still dark.

The final denial is further intensified when a whole group of bystanders, and no longer just a single person—and a maid at that—uncover Peter's identity.[13] It is not clear what gives Peter away, but regional accent or linguistic style or cultural patterns may have provided the clue. Perhaps, in a company of people where characteristic behavior calls for shoulder-rubbing intimacy, Peter remained isolated. At any rate, Peter's original vehemence now repeats itself and is echoed in the invocation of a curse on himself (14:71). From the initial denial of his association with Jesus the Nazarene to the final disavowal of any knowledge of "this man,"[14] the intensity of the repression mounts.

The "this man" of Mark might better be rendered in our usage as "that guy." In any case, the expression is a derogatory one, indicating a cultural signal of contempt. In the counseling world, the choice of words is treated very seriously. Often a genuine clue to meaning intended is found through reflection on the kinds of words chosen.

In this denial incident, Peter illustrates a classic portrayal of what Harry Stack Sullivan calls a "security operation." When a person's self-esteem is threatened so that anxiety results, appropriate behavior is replaced by attempts at defending the self. The stronger the attack, the more rigid the defense. The result is that most of a person's psychic energy is tied up in defensive maneuvers, leaving very little energy for constructive dealing with the situation. The more the maid pressed Peter, the more vehement his denial became.

The journalist Jhan Robbins reports on witnessing Dag Hammarskjöld, the late secretary-general of the United Nations, deal with a security operation on the streets of New York City at the height of the evening rush hour. Hammarskjöld was riding in Robbins' old red Jeep. It was an unexpected meeting, and Robbins was somewhat embarrassed to have his distinguished guest riding in the vehicle which he usually used only on his farm, but Robbins had missed his train that morning and had driven the Jeep into New York. Chugging along uptown in rush-hour traffic on the way to dinner, Robbins suddenly found a taxi cutting across his bow, forcing him to turn the Jeep onto the sidewalk, sideswiping a metal waste container which clanged like Big Ben. As the Jeep came to a halt against a lamppost, the taxi driver came striding over toward Robbins. Before he reached the Jeep, Robbins initiated the following dialogue:

Robbins:	Why didn't you signal! Couldn't you see you were cutting me off? What kind of a fool driver are you?
Cabby:	What do you mean by all that blasted honking? What's the matter, you blind or something? Where's your brains? Lemme see your license!
Robbins:	And let me see yours!
Cabby:	These days they give licenses to everybody. Even guys like you!
Robbins:	You could have killed us all, you maniac!
Cabby:	*(turning from Robbins to Hammarskjöld)* If I was you, I wouldn't ride with this guy. He's just a country driver—him and that jeep shoulda stayed in the sticks where they belong.
Hammarskjöld:	It must be tough driving a cab all day everyday in this town. I'm glad I don't have to do it—I couldn't stand it. I'm surprised there aren't more accidents!
Cabby:	Yeah, it is tough. If it isn't the other drivers, it's the snow or the rain or the cops or the trucks. You can't win. It's always tough driving in this town.
Robbins:	It sure is tough. I'm glad I don't have to drive here more than a couple of times a month.
Hammarskjöld:	*(turning to Robbins)* I'm sure your job has its hazards, too.
Robins:	I guess I was rattled, having you in the jeep, sir. Maybe I was a little careless.
Hammarskjöld:	*(turning to Cabby)* My friend feels he may have been a little careless.
Cabby:	Aw, maybe I did crowd him. I suppose I should have realized he was an out-of-town driver. He probably don't understand New York signals. *(to Robbins)* I guess we both got to watch out a little sharper.[15]

Hammarskjöld knew how to make it clear to people that they did not need to go on the defensive to call up their security operations.

Admitting need

The third issue is the power of remembrance. The crowing of the cock, which signals the coming of the day, brings with it the remembrance of Jesus' earlier prediction. The denials occur in different shades of darkness of night. Remembrance brings confrontation with self, in the light of the new day.[16]

Peter's weeping was the beginning of his growth into strength. The picture of Peter in Acts is that of a strong, effective leader. It was not his declaration of loyalty that made possible his growth; it was his admission of weakness. In a strange but powerful way, demonstrations of strength set people apart, repel closeness or intimacy, whereas open recognition of need, of weakness, brings people closer. The fulfillment of Jesus' prediction brought new hope, even in the valley of tears.[17]

Among men in much of the Western world, tears are often looked upon as a sign of weakness. But in Latin America, the Pacific Islands, and many other cultures, tears are simply a commonly accepted way of expressing both sorrow and joy. Whereas tears can be called forth for effect and can be seen as negative, they are more commonly simply an expression of strong feelings and, as such, can be tremendously therapeutic.[18]

Peter's salvation came through his tears. His first step toward growth into truly adult structure came when he deserted his bravado stance (his security operation) and wept. The Greek word is *epiballein*[19] which means "throw or cast upon; lay on," or "throw oneself upon, fall upon." In this sense, by his tears, Peter gave up his defenses and threw himself upon the mercy of God.

The therapeutic world provides some striking illustrations of the change that comes about when a person stops fighting (gives up a security operation), acknowledges problems, and admits needing help. In *Critical Incidents in Psychotherapy,* a case is presented of an inmate in prison, Tom, who was characterized by a social worker as "probably the most hopeless individual I have ever seen."[20] The clinical psychologist who had Tom in a therapy group found that Tom was destroying the group with his violent, immoderate, destructive behavior. When he called Tom in and confronted him with the possibility of dropping him from the group, Tom acted in his usual manner. The psychologist reports: "Still in a mocking manner, Tom stated that he had gotten nothing out of the group, that it was all an evident farce, that the other prisoners were giving me a 'snow job' [that is, were dishonestly pulling my leg], and that if I preferred I should send him out of the group."[21] After sparring a bit, the psychologist said to Tom that he would have to leave the group. The report goes on: "At this point Tom looked me in the eye and very clearly and slowly said, 'If you give me up, then there is no hope for me.' " The psychologist then writes:

> At this moment I was overwhelmed with a complex and powerful set of emotions composed of sorrow, hatred, pity and inadequacy. This sentence of Tom's became a "critical incident" for me. I was at that moment closer to him than I had ever been to any person on earth.[22]

Tom did leave the group, but the psychologist saw him individually for a considerable period of time. Tom eventually was relased and became a constructive, contributing member of society. The psychologist remarks that he felt he had become a "significant other" for Tom at the point that Tom had dropped his defenses and admitted his need.

CHAPTER SEVEN / WASHING

[JOHN 13:1-15]

JOHN'S GOSPEL IS full of surprises. In his hands, very ordinary events take on extraordinary meaning. A drink of water at a well becomes an occasion for teaching about how meaning can be found in life (4:1-42).[1] A woman caught in the act of adultery becomes an opportunity for pointing out how much guilt each person experiences (8:2-11). And the washing of feet at a meal becomes the occasion for dealing with death and separation (this passage, 13:1-15).

Foot-washing is a powerfully symbolic act. Like symbols in general, this act has a specific, immediate meaning and a broad, ultimate meaning. It was common in ancient Palestinian culture, an act of courtesy performed routinely, but it was far more than that. It was also an act symbolizing the need for cleansing at a deeper level.[2] The act, and the record and reflection on the act, show up as the two sides of this story. As in every story of John's Gospel, the act is the "sign" or the "work" Jesus did; for it to be meaningful for those who first saw or experienced it, it had to have some reference, some context, in that person's (or group's) culture or everyday life experience. By interpreting the act and by having it written down to be read, it becomes a symbolic sign for readers at any time when the sense of the story is associated with reference to the readers' life and world.

John's story of the foot-washing[3] describes an effort by Jesus at creating a special kind of climate. The disciples didn't offer to Jesus or to one another this needed and welcome service; and Jesus himself is filled with an awareness accentuating the chasm between him and them. One can only infer from parallels in the Synoptics, from passages dealing with the disciples' concern for "who is the greatest among us?"[4] that Jesus needed to teach them by reminding them that the Son of man did not come to be served but to serve. But unlike the Synoptics, where Jesus only teaches about this point, here in John he does something to change the very atmosphere which was too detrimental for anything positive to happen.

In working to create a favorable climate, Jesus was doing what any alert counselor or educator or administrator tries to do. In the counseling world, a high priority is given to establishing a climate conducive to growth. The attention that Jesus showed toward creating a positive climate was typical of his way of dealing with people. It is also typical of most truly effective therapists. One therapist who paid a good deal of attention to the kind of climate in which he could work was the psychiatrist Harry Stack Sullivan. Sullivan believed that matters of self-esteem lay at the root of most problems in interpersonal relationships. He therefore set himself to the task of never undermining his patients' sense of self-esteem. Or, expressed positively, he reinforced his patients' self-esteem on every occasion possible.

Sullivan displayed an underlying optimism about what could be accomplished, even with quite sick persons. He believed that the most effective force leading to change in interpersonal relationships was a positive appraisal from a significant person. He reminded his students that in every interpersonal contact, an influence was exerted that could, on the one hand, affirm, underscore, and reinforce feelings of self-esteem; or, on the other hand, could deny, undercut, and undermine such feelings. He placed special importance on the power of positive reflected appraisals as found in a chum in the preadolescent stage, but he saw such appraisals as operating at every stage of life.[5]

By the foot-washing, Jesus changed the climate at the supper. He did it by assuming the humble role of a servant. Significant as the example of humility was, it is not the central message of this passage. As elsewhere in John's Gospel, Jesus moves from an act with concrete reference in a concrete context to a symbolic meaning.[6] The need for purification, which only Jesus perceives as he enters into the foot-washing, becomes an issue.[7] Without such washing, there will be no partnership, no friendship, no inheritance, no having a share in him.

This passage has a special cultural reference, signaled by the mention of the Passover (13:1). At Passover, Jews were and are accustomed to preparing themselves for its symbolic significance by purifying themselves (11:55). For the disciples to experience getting cleansed (i.e., having feet washed), and to take it as "example" to do to one another is parallel to the need for their drinking of the same cup that Jesus must drink, and for their being baptized with the same baptism he will be baptized with (Matt. 20:22, Mark 10:38-39). While Peter's argumentative reply in 13:6-9 is in tone and substance identical to that in Mark 8:31-33 after Jesus gave his first "passion prediction," the subsequent instruction about true discipleship, in John as in the Synoptics, confronts the disciples with the need to share in Jesus' death. By sharing in his death, they will be released to love and to service. There are four issues in this passage we wish to consider.

Leaving and returning

In this passage, leave-taking from the disciples is dealt with not by itself but in the context of returning to God. Both emphases are touched on in verse 1, which refers both to "his hour" (of leaving) and to "the end" (return to God).

Leave-taking, for John, is related to the hour of glorification. Just as Luke takes the travel section dealt with in Mark and Matthew and expands it into a major concern,[8] so John develops the separation by death into the theme of having a share in Jesus by going all the way with him—even to the cross. This, for John, is the "hour of glorification," for not until then is it "finished."

It is only in recent times that we have begun to appreciate the importance of leave-taking.[9] The gospel record is full of instances in which Jesus takes temporary leave from those with whom he associates. We believe that much of this leave-taking was quite intentional, a preparation for the day when his presence would be less tangible or visible than people were used to. His withdrawals forced certain issues that might otherwise never have been broached. Just as any counselor presses in on some occasions and holds back on others, so Jesus used his periodic separations as a part of his therapeutic strategy. He recognized how much resistance there would be to his relinquishing his role as their leader, and so he set about preparing them for it. Like most people in our own day, the disciples did not want to think about the possibility of separation.

When we think of how many times any one of us needs to say good-bye to loved ones and associates, whether in permanent or temporary separation, the importance of leave-taking becomes more obvious. Jesus kept raising the issue of his leaving because he recognized how essential it was to help his disciples and friends work through the severing of their relationship with him. Virtually every leave-taking needs opportunity for open discussion of the meaning of the impending separation, and this is true whether the feelings about separation are positive or negative.

But leave-taking for Jesus is more than the sorrow of separation. He interprets his death as a liberating experience, both for himself and for his disciples. His death is a service for his disciples, just as washing their feet is a service to them.[10] They have called him "Teacher and Lord" (13:13), thus stressing a seemingly unbridgeable distance between them and him, but he performs an act of service which bridges the distance and makes possible an equality in friendship.

In the beginning, Jesus was a teacher to his disciples, but in this passage he assumes the role of servant. Later in John's Gospel, Jesus calls his disciples "friends" (15:15).[11] In still another place he refers to them as "children" (21:5). Since we have been asserting that the words chosen for communication are important, we cannot simply dismiss the matter of the choice of names as insignificant. But the different choice of name came at quite different occasions. It was as if Jesus recognized that sometimes his disciples needed to be able to lean on him as teacher, but that on other occasions they could relate to him as friend. Sometimes they were like immature children in his presence, but other times they were recognized as well-functioning adults.

It is common in counseling work to find people making progress toward adultlike living only to slip back into infantile ways. On one occasion a counselee needs to be affirmed for mature and constructive achievement, but on other occasions the support of a nurturing counselor may be very much in order. It is characteristic of growth that it comes in spurts and that progress today may lead to regression tomorrow.

Jesus understood that his disciples would have difficulty in seeing anything but loss in his separation from them. We find his understanding stressed in the words spoken to Peter: "What I am doing you do not know now, but afterwards you will understand" (13:7). It is characteristic of John to have us experience a sign that has a sensory dimension to it,[12] yet the substance of what was experienced sensorily can be perceived only by faith. The deeper, the true (eternal) meaning of such acts is accessible only to the believer, as we are repeatedly told throughout the gospel, and as is twice more emphasized in the conclusion: once in the "doubting Thomas" story (20:20-28), and then immediately following in the summary (20:31, see also 19:35).

Empowering in relating to God

The second issue is one of empowerment. Jesus found his identity in his relationship with God. He was empowered by this relationship, both for the immediate concerns of everyday life (taking the towel) and for the ultimate issues (going to the cross). Again and again in his ministry he referred people to God. Whether it was with the Samaritan woman (4:4-27) or Nicodemus (3:1-21), the message was the same: line up your life with God's purposes. In the case of Jesus, verses 3 and 4 put it very clearly: "Jesus, knowing . . . that he had come from God and was going to God . . . girded himself with a towel."

Empowerment is also a concern for us. The example in the story consists not merely of a reflection on what Jesus is (= to believe that Jesus is the Christ, the Son of God), but also on what we are or are to become (= in believing have life in his name): empowered to become children of God (John 1:12); to become his friends.

This orientation invites a double focus: one on the present and one on the future. There is a sense in which we all are always both "being" and "becoming." Just how the present is related to the future is often unclear, but the relationship is there. Thornton Wilder wrote a novel, *The Eighth Day,* which has been called a book written in the resurrection mode. It ends suddenly in the middle of a sentence, without any punctuation. It is as if the novelist is saying, "You write the ending. It is your story too. You finish it."

In one graphic scene in *The Eighth Day,* a large tapestry is examined on its back side. No design can be discerned in the tangle of knotted threads. But when the tapestry is turned over so that the front is revealed, there is an intricate design with every thread participating in and contributing to the design. Life is like a tapestry, Wilder is saying, and a design is there, even though it is revealed or becomes accessible only to the "eye" of the believer.

Wilder has the same fundamental optimism that characterizes the Christian (and the Jewish) biblical faith. The Johannine Jesus is aware of having descended from God and was ascending to God, yet in that ascent there was a new descent: the coming of the Spirit, taking hold of us to assure that Jesus and the Father make their dwelling with us (14:23). Likewise Wilder is convinced that life is lived in the presence of God. He notes that God created humanity on the sixth day and rested on the seventh. "We are at the beginning of the second week. We are children of the eighth day."[13]

Integrating the bad and the good

The third issue involves the integration of the bad with the good. Verse 2 describes an ominous force at work in the midst of the disciples, which John 13:2 describes as "the devil had already put it in to the heart of Judas to betray," that is, to abandon Christ altogether. Judas, though washed, remains "not clean" (13:11); he stands symbolically for the presence of the unredeemed, for the element of what C. G. Jung would call the shadow.[14] Throughout this brief passage the presence of this irreconcilable force of evil is noted (13:2, 10-11; see also 18:32). The role of Judas here is not to represent moral evil, but symbolically he represents that which does not become integrated and hence will not "inherit." The reaction to Peter is reminiscent of the encounter at Caesarea Philippi: "Get behind me, Satan!"[15] The diabolic spirit is always present, whether in Peter or in Judas, ready to take over if given a chance, "like a roaring lion, seeking some one to devour" (I Peter 5:8).

Thornton Wilder gives an everyday illustration of the need to integrate the bad along with the good in *The Eighth Day*. Eustacia Lansing struggled much of her married life with envy. She envied her friend Beata who was married to John Ashley, a wonderfully understanding and loving partner, while she was married to a petty tyrant. It was one night in Fort Barry after John Ashley had proved once again to be a friend in time of need, that Eustacia sat for a long hour in the dark, contemplating her life.

During that hour she ridded herself—threw overboard—the last remnants of an unhappiness that had long tormented her—she ceased to envy Beata Ashley her marriage. . . . At Fort Barry she divested herself of the last pangs of envy.[16]

Providing an example

The fourth issue, stressed in the last verses of the passage, is the example provided by Jesus. The power of an example has seldom been demonstrated more graphically than in this washing of the disciples' feet. Rather than depending on verbal instruction, Jesus chose to act out his teaching. In an active, involved way he made his point, rising from the supper table, laying aside his outer clothes, girding himself with a towel, pouring water into a basin, and proceeding to wash his disciples' feet. The action must have been all the more impressive when it took place "during the supper." This more-than-verbal demonstration was then underscored with a verbal accent: "I have given you an example" (13:15). Literally, foot-washing was done to saints as expression of hospitality;[17] figuratively, it is the manifestation of a new social order rooted in sacrificial love. The same idea is expressed in John 15:12-17 about laying down one's life for one's friend, about bearing fruit which abides.

For the helping person who perceives the helping role as one largely of consulting-room dialogue, this demonstration offers a specific challenge. Indeed, the ministry of Jesus offers innumerable illustrations of more-than-verbal actions that complement teachings. Whether it involved driving out the money-changers (2:13-16) or feeding the five thousand (6:1-14) or riding on a donkey (12:14), Jesus employed a wide variety of nonverbal approaches to drive home his message.

A powerful example was found in the life pattern of Harry Stack Sullivan. He is one of the therapists who was most aware of the place of the more-than-verbal dimension in treatment. His own life was an example of deep concern for people and deep commitment to ideals. Most of his early days as a psychiatrist were spent with patients on the back wards of mental hospitals—patients largely given up by others. He had an amazing capacity to make contact with patients who were apparently unreachable. His success in reaching the unreachable was legendary.

Sullivan died of a heart attack as he was returning from a meeting of the World Mental Health Organization. His doctors had warned him to slow down, but he had such a sense of urgency for sharing on an international scale what the psychiatric world had discovered in personal relationships that he gave himself without reservation to the interests of world peace. At his memorial service, a colleague spoke these words: "Here was the finest example of social responsibility, unselfish devotion and true maturity that any of us is likely ever to see."[18] Sullivan himself wrote of his own goal: "Begin; and let it be said of you, if there is any more history, that you labored nobly in the measure of man in the XX Century of the scientific, Western World."[19]

Effective as his example was, Sullivan nevertheless believed in using the verbal medium to underscore what had been demonstrated nonverbally. He was quite insistent on the need to put into words the point that is being stressed.[20] In similar manner, Jesus reinforced what he had done by calling attention to it as an example.

It is instructive that Jesus ends the incident of washing his disciples' feet with a call to action. And the call is not only to the specific concern of washing one another's feet. It is also the call to constant vigilance in keeping the channels open to God, in holding the forces of evil at bay, in practicing service. It is reminiscent of the closing verses of John's Gospel when Peter is enjoined three times to "feed my sheep," and alerted that he will get carried where he does not wish to go (21:15-19).

Chapter Eight / Preparing

●

THROUGHOUT THE NEW Testament we have noted how often events have a surprise ending. Nowhere is this more true than in the resurrection story as recorded in Mark 16:1-8. Three women going to the tomb to anoint the body of Jesus for burial find, to their utter surprise, that the tomb is open (not sealed by its massive stone) and that the body is not there. Instead of Jesus, the women find an angel who declares: "He has risen, he is not here . . . he is going before you to Galilee" (16:6, 7). The implication is, "He is still preparing the way."

Once again we are confronted with a choice: read the story as a factual, historical record, but then go on to read the passage through the eyes of faith. As a historical record, the story makes little sense. As a testimony of faith, it states the central truth of Christianity. Fritz Kunkel notes that the real ending of the Gospel of Mark is at 16:8[1] (before the appearance of Jesus) and comments: "History itself sees to it that Christianity be based on faith and not on historical evidence."[2]

The central motive in Mark's Gospel can be expressed in an imperative: Prepare the way of the Lord! When Mark writes in 1:1 of "the beginning of the gospel," a pathway and a goal are implied. The gospel is the story of being on the way with Jesus. It begins with the Old Testament admonition, "Prepare the way of the Lord" (1:3). Even at the tomb, the message is still one of preparing the way. The young man in the tomb declares: "Jesus of Nazareth"[3] "is going before you" (16:6, 7). Death does not stop the process. The way of the Lord has been prepared, but further preparation is still needed.

There are three aspects of preparing the way that we want to examine.

Doing grief work

The resurrection story begins with three women going to the tomb, ready to carry on their task of preparing the body of Jesus for burial. Presumably there had not been time to anoint[4] the body with spices after Joseph of Arimathea had laid it in the tomb and had sealed the entrance with a heavy stone. They thought that they were doing a routine task, that is, doing their grief work in the performance of a tangible act of service which would help them come to terms with their grief. It was their very willingness to do the work of grieving that made it possible for them to move beyond their grief.

There is no substitute for the work of grieving. Arthur Miller wrote with deep psychological insight when he has his character Quentin say: "You never stop loving whoever you loved."[5] The work of mourning is never easy. To come to terms with the loss of a significant person takes an enormous amount of energy, involves carrying out many tangible tasks that help evoke memories, and includes a reliving of the events that helped build the relationship. All of this was involved as the women went to the tomb. Because they were in the process of doing their grief work, they were freer than the fleeing disciples to hear the message of hope.

The challenge for the women, as for us, is how to be open to new dimensions in life without getting caught in old routines, such as carrying ointments to the tomb. For the most part, doing routine work helps in the work of grieving. But routine itself can become a trap. Mark stressed over and over again how easily people are caught in familiar routines, unwilling to try anything different. It is not possible to say how long it takes to do the work of mourning. Some people are able to work through their grief quite rapidly, but for others the process is much longer. Generally speaking, the work of grieving is measured not in days but in months. Grieving is hard, and it takes a good deal of time. But grieving needs to be done.

Because the women were willing to begin their grief work in a tangible act of service, a whole new dimension of life opened up before them with a fresh start. This fresh start, this new beginning is signaled by the words of the second verse: "And very early on the first day of the week they went to the tomb when the sun had risen" (16:2). Thornton Wilder gives one of his novels the title *The Eighth Day*. His reference is to the first day after the creation of the world had been completed, the time when man and woman were called upon to go to work.

> The process of life never stands still. The creation has not come to an end. The Bible says that God created man on the sixth day and rested, but each of those days was many millions of years long. That day of rest must have been a short one. Man is not an end but a beginning. We are at the beginning of the second week. We are children of the eighth day.[6]

In doing the work of grieving, the women were doing sixth-day work, but it made possible for them the beginning of the eighth day.

It is instructive that the first "very early" visitors to the tomb were women. The word of the resurrection came first not to men but to women. Is it because women are more tuned to the intuitive realm of life, more open than men to the symbolic dimension? Fritz Kunkel believes so as he writes in *Creation Continues:*

> The women, carrying the mystery of unending life within themselves, are more ready than men to respond to the mystery of metaphysical rebirth. The grave, the womb of mother earth, as the cradle of spiritual life, to them is but another higher form of their own experience of motherhood.[7]

75

Using fear

The primary reaction of the women to finding the open tomb was one of fear: "They were afraid" (16:8). Initially their reaction was one of amazement. They were amazed to find that the stone had been rolled away. They were amazed at the startling sight of a young man sitting in the tomb[8] dressed in a white robe.[9] They were amazed at the young man's message. They were astonished over the entire event, and their astonishment turned to fear (16:8).

In Mark's Gospel there are a number of references to fear. These references commonly relate to a reaction coming in the presence of unknown forces and are related to faith. So in 4:39-40, Jesus calms the seas and then relates the fear of the disciples to their lack of faith. In 5:33 the woman with a flow of blood who came to Jesus in fear and trembling is healed because of her faith. In 10:32 the disciples were "amazed and . . . afraid." For the women in the resurrection passage to react with "trembling and astonishment"[10] is the characteristic way of reacting in the biblical record to revelation.

It is significant that the record notes that the women "fled from the tomb . . . and . . . said nothing to anyone" (16:8). Their fear was so great that, although they could run off, they could not bring themselves to tell anyone what they had seen and heard. Unable to integrate the presence of the angel and his message, they did nothing with it. Their fear[11] was so great that it paralyzed them into inactivity.

Repression of fear is a common experience. Mark records an incident in which the disciples did not understand what Jesus had said, and "were afraid to ask him" (9:32).[12] Jesus, who had been talking about his impending death, knew that his disciples were repressing their anxieties about his leaving them. Like any good therapist, he encouraged them to talk about what they had feared to bring up with him. His implication was that no matter how "scary" the subject was, it could be talked about. He brought out into the open something which, out of fear, they had kept to themselves.

Much of the depth therapy of the psychiatric world is devoted to bringing into the open that which has been repressed into the unconscious, usually out of anxiety. Dr. M. Scott Peck gives a detailed account of a man who called himself Ted, who described his inability to get moving into anything by saying: "Life seems to be an insurmountable problem."[13] After long hours of analytic work, it became apparent that Ted was really a deeply religious person who had repressed his religious impulses because of early ridicule from his family. With the help of Dr. Peck, he was able to accept his natural inclination and enter theological school. Dr. Peck noted that Ted now signed his name "Theodore" and commented on it. Theodore wrote back:

> I was hoping you would notice it. . . . When I was very young my Aunt told me that I should be proud of the name Theodore because it means "lover of God." I was proud. So I told my brothers about it. . . . Did they make fun of me. They called me a sissy in ten different ways. . . . So I became embarrassed by the name. A few weeks ago it occurred to me that I was no longer embarrassed. So I decided it was all right to use my full name now. After all, I am a lover of God, aren't I?[14]

Peck summarizes what had happened: "Ted's forsaken belief in God had to be resurrected as an essential part of the liberation and resurrection of his spirit."[15] Embarrassment had paralyzed Ted for many years, resulting in an inability to handle life. Fear paralyzed the women at the tomb, at least temporarily.

Viktor Frankl likes to emphasize that everyone can be helped, but that often the help comes in unexpected ways. The grief of the women was met not as they had expected but in a new, constructive challenge. The answer to their sorrow was to be found not just by grieving, but by relating to Jesus in an entirely new way.

Getting involved

The third emphasis in the passage is the call to involvement in Galilee. The women had been with Jesus in Galilee (15:41). To go back to Galilee is to continue their preparation for being "on the way." Galilee is the symbol for ongoing life, whereas Jerusalem is the symbol for crucifixion and death. The young man at the tomb does not send the disciples back to Jerusalem but speaks of their seeing Jesus in Galilee. The very ones who deserted Jesus, the disciples who were appointed "to be with him," and the very one who denied him—Peter, "the Rock"—are to be reminded that Jesus can be seen in Galilee. Indeed, the message is stronger than that: "You *will* see him" (16:7 which reiterates 14:28): women, disciples, and Peter. As any communicator knows, an important message needs to be given more than once.

The three women were already involved with Jesus, but this involvement had been as those who had looked on "from afar" (15:40). They were involved, but their involvement was at a distance.[16] They were attracted to Jesus, but they were disappointed and angry and withheld themselves from him. The admonition of the young man for them to be with Jesus again in Galilee is the call to return to where Jesus first proclaimed "the gospel of God" (1:14). But everything is changed now, so that the call is really for a deeper involvement, a more personal and a more communal commitment. The question now is, How much of their lives will be lived in the light of the eighth day, and how much will be bound up in grieving "from afar"?

The act of going to "tell his disciples and Peter"[17] that "he is going before you to Galilee" (16:7) means getting involved in a very personal and interpersonal way. But according to the narrator, the women, out of fear and trembling, "said nothing." Alan Paton wrote a powerful novel of South Africa entitled *Too Late the Phalarope*. The very first page of the book describes a situation in which a refusal to get involved led to tragic consequences:

Perhaps I could have saved him, with only a word, two words, out of my mouth. Perhaps I could have saved us all. But I never spoke them. . . .

For he spoke hard and bitter words to me, and shut the door of his soul on me, and I withdrew. But I should have hammered on it, I should have broken it down with my naked hands, I should have cried out there not ceasing, for behind it was a man in danger, the bravest and gentlest of them all. . . . Because of the power he had over me, I *held*, in the strange words of the English, *I held my peace*.[18]

We can sympathize with this woman, who, in "fear and trembling" held her peace and withheld her involvement. Like the women at the tomb, she had been confronted with something new (in her case, rejection in "hard and bitter words"), and like them she reacted by withdrawing, by doing nothing. We all know what it is to be afraid when our known world is challenged and disturbed. We know how anxious we become when we are asked to do something we haven't done before. We know how anxious we become when we are asked to grow beyond where we are, to become more deeply involved in a way of life that leads to a new and unknown place. Fear and trembling is a part of our lives too.

The "fear and trembling" of the women describes their mood, but it does not define the outcome of the story. These women went to the tomb knowing that it would be closed, but they went anyway. A realistic appraisal of the situation was that they couldn't get into the tomb without help, but they went in spite of that. What they were attempting was impossible, but they attempted it nonetheless.

What happened was that an entirely unexpected element entered the picture. It is as if the women went, open to the possibility of the impossible happening. Because they went, their whole lives were redirected into unexpected patterns. The transformation in their lives, and in the lives of the disciples, speaks of the power of God at work in life. Paul puts it very succinctly: "Work out your own salvation with fear and trembling: for God is at work in you" (Phil. 2:12-13).

CHAPTER NINE / REJOICING

[I PETER 1:3-9]

TO REJOICE IN TRIALS simply doesn't make sense to most people. But to rejoice in difficult times, to welcome hardships, is the mark of a Christian, so Peter declares in I Peter 1:3-9. This surprising affirmation is presented as the basis for hope.[1]

In this letter Peter both identifies himself with the Christians he is writing to ("*we* have been born anew," 1:3) and sets himself apart as one who can speak authoritatively to them ("Peter an apostle of Jesus Christ. . . . In this *you* rejoice," 1:1; 1:6, etc.).[2] The letter is one of the seven "general" or "catholic" letters written not to a specific person or church but rather to Christians in general, exiles of the dispersion.[3] The five provinces, basically in Asia Minor, are listed in the order in which the bearer of a circular letter would travel.

In the old liturgical lectionary, I Peter 1:3-9 was a reading for the first Sunday following Easter, when new members of the faith were baptized and instructed about integrated living. The passage expresses the substance of the whole range of issues covered between Easter and the end of the church year. Central in Peter's thought is hope. It is hope that gives meaning to suffering, whether in the trials of living as "exiles of the Dispersion" (1:1) across the ancient world or in enduring the problems of living in any age.

There are four issues we want to deal with in this passage.

Revealing God as an active force

The first issue in this passage is the description of God as a force at work in our lives.[4] This is a force that generates power in two ways: in the historical work of salvation in the death and resurrection of Jesus (1:3), and in the future aspect of "the coming" *(parousia)* of Jesus at his "apocalypse" (1:4-5).[5] Both aspects suggest a new quality of life for us, both in the sense of facing life in a new perspective (children of the eighth day, in Wilder's term)[6] and in the sense of anticipating an even greater potential that is still to come. The apocalypse, psychologically, refers to the most complete kind of self-fulfillment.[7]

It is often in terms of suffering that God is seen most clearly at work. John Marsh writes of the impact of the writings of the German theologian Karl Barth just before World War II.

> I was in Germany in the early days of 1938 on the very day when the second volume of his great *Dogmatik* was delivered in the post of the German Confessional Pastor with whom I was staying. It was as if a year's supply of food had come to some beleaguered city that would otherwise have starved to death. I shall never forget the joy and delight of that morning post; and I have never since been able to give much credence to critics who, from a safe and comfortable Anglo-American study armchair, tell the world that Barth's theology is theoretical and remote.[8]

Marsh summarizes Barth's message: "to leave completely undistorted and uncompromised the great, wonderful and mysterious fact that God has spoken to us in his son, Jesus Christ our Lord."[9] Marsh notes that "Barth made the churches of Germany face some most searching and awkward questions about the duty of the Church under a tyrant like Hitler."[10] Here God was seen to be at work through Karl Barth.

Rejoicing in spite of suffering

The second issue is the paradox of new birth. The new birth, which represents a discontinuity with the readers' own past and with this current situation as exiles in the dispersion, generates two things: something causing rejoicing and something causing anxiety. The something causing rejoicing (1:6, 8) is "a living hope" (1:3), "an inheritance . . . kept in heaven" (1:4), "a salvation ready to be revealed in the last time" (1:5). The something causing anxiety is the suffering of "various trials" (1:6).[11] The paradox lies in the combining of rejoicing and anxiety.

The historical element in this paradox is the death and resurrection of Jesus. The symbolic element is in the parousia,[12] the promise of fulfillment of potentiality in the future. Viewed both historically and symbolically, rejoicing is combined with anxiety. In Christianity the two are irreversibly intertwined.

Psychiatrist M. Scott Peck begins his book *The Road Less Traveled* with these words: "Life is difficult." He goes on to write that real joy (rejoicing) comes only when the problems of life (anxiety) are handled. "Since life poses an endless series of problems, life is always difficult and full of pain as well as joy."[13] Gordon Allport, probably America's foremost psychologist,[14] taught for most of his professional life at Harvard University. Allport never subscribed to the major trends of psychoanalytic thinking which dominated American psychology for several decades in the middle of the twentieth century. He believed that the people who found this way into the most joyous kind of living (rejoicing) voluntarily chose a way of life that created problems (anxiety). He cites the experience of James Bryant Conant on the occasion of being inaugurated as president of Harvard College.

> Conant remarked that he was undertaking his duties "with a heavy heart but gladly." He knew he would reduce no tension by committing himself to the new job. Tensions

would mount and mount, and at many times become almost unbearable. While he would in the course of his daily work dispatch many tasks and feel relief, still the over-all commitments—his total investment of energy—would never result in any equilibrium.[15]

Allport goes on to note that human interests are of the kind that lead us "to complicate and strain our lives indefinitely."[16] It is normal for healthy adults to combine rejoicing with anxiety.

All four of the psychological writers that we have been citing stress the struggle (anxiety)[17] involved in growth (rejoicing). Viktor Frankl declares: "What counts . . . is to turn one's predicament into a human achievement.[18] C. G. Jung asserts: "There is no coming to consciousness without pain."[19] Harry Stack Sullivan notes how the patient needs to be helped in the struggle to change:

> He has to be led to observe closely, to catch on to the exact functional activity concerned—the "personal use" of belief to him; then to see that the formula is by no means the best for achieving a useful end; and only then can he go about using his abilities to be "more realistic," less defensively vulnerable, in the field of collaboration.[20]

Virginia Satir affirms: "Some human pain is unavoidable, of course. But as a people, we don't always put our efforts in the right place, to change what we can and to work out creative ways to live with what we can't change."[21]

When Peter writes that "though now for a little while you may have to suffer various trials" (1:6), he is thinking especially of the problem of living as political exiles. Kim Chi Ha, called by some South Korea's leading literary figure, has been imprisoned many times for his outspoken opposition, as a Christian, to the political regime of Park Chung Hee in South Korea. From prison he writes a letter to the National Priests Association for the Realization of Justice:

> Praise to the Lord!
> How are you all? Thanks to the Lord's mercy and your prayers, I am fine.

I am in solitary confinement in a dark cell and forbidden to write or read, even Scripture. I spend each day in meditation, surrounded by these gloomy walls. Nonetheless, my spirits are closer to the Lord than ever before. . . . As long as the Lord is at my side and you continue your dauntless movement out there, I have no misgivings about this tribulation the Lord has presented to me as a sign of his divine will.[22]

Kim Chi Ha rejoices in spite of his suffering.

Testing faith repeatedly

Our third issue is that suffering tests faith. Just as rejoicing is the outcome of faith, so suffering, whether unexpected or not, serves to test the genuineness of faith. And this testing may be for an individual or, as in the case of I Peter, for a group. Faith that is tested has a goal ("outcome," 1:9) and promise which is the living hope, the inheritance.

Arthur Miller wrote a play called *The Crucible*[23] which deals with the theme of "faith, more precious than gold which though perishable is tested by fire" (1:7). A crucible, the hollow at the bottom of a furnace which receives melted metal after imperfections have been burned off, is defined as "something that tests affliction, as if by fire; a severe test or trial."[24] It is in the fires of affliction, Miller is saying, that true character is revealed. Proctor, the leading actor in the play, has been persuaded to admit that he saw the devil and did "bind" himself "to the devil's service." But when the court had him sign his confession, intending to post it publicly for all to see, he tore the paper up and renounced his confession. Reverend Hale, the prosecutor, speaks to Proctor:

Hale: Man, you will hang! You cannot!
Proctor: *(his eyes full of tears)* I can. And there's your first marvel, that I can. You have made your magic now, for now I do think I see some shred of goodness in John Proctor. Not enough to weave a banner with, but white enough to keep it from such dogs.[25]

Thus in the final moment John Proctor makes his stand, refuses to give in to the lie that would save his life, and goes to the gallows rejoicing. He is a changed man. He is like gold tested in the fire where the dross has been consumed. The gold is purified, changed. It is as if he was responding to the words of I Peter 5:8-9: "Your adversary the devil prowls around like a roaring lion, seeking someone to devour. Resist him, firm in your faith, knowing that the same experience of suffering is required of your brotherhood throughout the world."[26] The vivid imagery of the devil who "prowls around like a roaring lion" suggests that faith is tested not just occasionally but repeatedly.

Identifying followers of Christ

The fourth issue is found in the tests of genuine identity of Christ's followers. There are three tests (1:8). The first is in loving Christ "without having seen him."[27] The second is believing in Christ "though you do not now see him." The third is rejoicing "with unutterable and exalted joy," or, as Weymouth translates it, "you nevertheless trust, and triumph with a joy which is unspeakable and is crowned with glory."[28] These three tests are met by those who are in the process of developing (see 2:2, "grow up") from "new birth" to "inheritance" or "salvation," threatened though that development is (or was or will be) by various trials.

It was America's most famous psychologist, William James, who wrote of the feelings of joy and glory that characterize those who have been "twice born," who have experienced a dramatic conversion.[29] In *After the Fall*, Arthur Miller speaks to the same theme, but in the much more common experience of being helped in emotional growth. Quentin, a lawyer, has helped a dancer, Felice, through a divorce. Felice has said to Quentin: "I always wanted to tell you this—you changed my life!" Quentin muses: "I may stand in her mind like some important corner she turned in life. And she meant so little to me. I feel like a mirror in which she somehow saw herself as glorious."[30]

Felice saw herself as glorious not because of anything she had done, but because of the way Quentin treated her. She tells of how he affected her former husband. "The way you talked to him; it made him act so dignified I almost began to love him!"[31] Quentin had the capacity to call forth the best in a person.

Although it is a terrifying thought, we, on occasion, act for God. As I Peter puts it, it is "by his great mercy" that "we have been born anew to a living hope" (1:3). Being born anew is not something that we do for ourselves. It is something done for us by God, or by those who act for God. Virginia Satir is very clear about what makes a person feel glorious: "Feelings of worth can only flourish in an atmosphere where individual differences are appreciated, mistakes are tolerated, communications open and rules are flexible."[32] It is our unique opportunity to create such an atmosphere and thus to act for God.

Chapter Ten / Enabling

THE STORY OF PENTECOST is the story of the surprising mixture of the ordinary with the extraordinary, of the usual with the unusual, of the normal with the abnormal. For people to come together in a house was ordinary. But for these same people to leave fired up with enthusiasm was extraordinary. For people to talk together was usual. But for the same people to be enabled to talk in strange languages and still be understood was unusual. To hear the sound of the wind is normal, but to report that "a sound came from heaven like a rush of a mighty wind" (2:2) is abnormal.

This is not the first place in the Bible that ordinary and extraordinary events are intermingled. When Moses was called from the prosaic work of keeping sheep to become God's messenger to lead the chosen people out of bondage in Egypt, there was the same mingling of the usual with the unusual. Elizabeth Barrett Browning describes the sense of the call of Moses vividly in four simple lines:

> . . . Earth's crammed with heaven
> and every common bush afire with God;
> But only he who sees takes off his shoes,
> The rest sit round it and pluck blackberries.[1]

The action in Acts 2:1-21 takes place at an ordinary place (a house, 2:2) at an extraordinary time (Pentecost, 2:1).[2] The place of normal social life is made abnormal by the presence of twelve different individuals: the historical

89

twelve minus Judas Iscariot, but replenished by newcomer Matthias, and perhaps also "all the others" (that is, "the women" and members of Jesus' family, 1:14). This group of people represents the remembrance of God's recent activity in their midst and their hopes of God's renewed activity, promised to them in Luke 24:49 and echoed in Acts 1:1 ("all that Jesus *began* to do and teach") and Acts 1:4-5.[3]

There are four aspects of the Pentecost account that we want to accent.

Empowering for action

The first is the empowering impact of the coming of the Holy Spirit. The passage gives a vivid description of the theophany (a divine manifestation), first in sound and then in sight. "Suddenly a sound came from heaven like the rush of a mighty wind, and it filled all the house where they were sitting" (2:2). In Mary Ellen Chase's novel *Windswept,* the old-country handyman tells how the strong wind reminds him of Pentecost: "I heard the wind last night. . . . It filled our house with sound. At once it made me think of the great wind which was the Holy Ghost of God. You remember, at Pentecost, like the Bible says."[4] Even more vivid is the imagery of sight. "And there appeared to them tongues as of fire, distributed and resting on each one of them" (2:3). The chorus of the Boston University School of Theology hymn picks up this same imagery:

> O crucified and risen Lord,
> Give tongues of fire to preach Thy Word.[5]

The impact of the coming of the Holy Spirit is reported in two ways. In the first place all were "filled with the Holy Spirit" (2:4). It is not clear whether the "all" refers only to the disciples or to the others as well (the women and the members of Jesus' family, see "all the house" in 2:2). In the second place the disciples began to speak "in other tongues as the Spirit gave them utterance."[6]

The rushing wind and the flames of fire are vivid metaphors stressing the empowering action of God. Mary Ellen Chase concludes her novel *Windswept* with the note of empowering. Like Elizabeth Barrett Browning, she saw "every common bush afire" in the Maine autumn scene and recalls Pentecost:

> The land glowed with patches of scarlet and crimson, rust and gold, above the green and purple sea. The flames at Pentecost, she thought, coming with a mighty rushing wind, still touching men so that they may speak in other tongues than their own, still enabling their sons and their daughters to prophesy, their young men to see visions and their old men to dream dreams.[7]

The enabling that she refers to stresses the continuing action of God: "*still* touching . . . *still* enabling." But only the men and women who are open to hearing the sound of the rushing wind or to seeing the flames of fire have their lives changed. As Elizabeth Barrett Browning puts it so graphically, only those who see take off their shoes; "the rest sit round . . . and pluck blackberries."

Overcoming barriers

The second aspect of the Pentecost account of particular interest is the emphasis on overcoming the barriers of language. "The mighty works of God" (2:11) were told in twelve different native languages, thus reaching those near (Jews and proselytes) and far (as far west as Rome; as far east as Parthia; as far south as northern Africa; as far north as the coast of the Black Sea). The breadth of the language facility thus spanned political, cultural, and ideological barriers—such as the Rome–Parthia rivalry, which led to the first-century superpower confrontation.[8]

There is sense in which the telling of the mighty works of God unites people across all barriers of time and place. I (RCL) recall being in Teheran in 1971 and preaching in a Methodist church on a Sunday (which was an ordinary working day there) with a translator to translate into

Persian. Even if there had been no translator, I believe our sense of unity as Christians was so great that communication would have taken place.

But language *is* a barrier. A psychiatrist from the United States who did research into mental illness among refugees in the new nation of Israel tells how in modern times there are "dwelling in Jerusalem Jews, devout men [and women] from every nation under heaven" (2:5). He tells of the almost insuperable problems the language barriers present to someone who is trying to do psychotherapy. The only thing the refugees had in common was the Jewish faith. One of the urgent needs was for some common way to communicate in words.

In our teaching at Pacific School of Religion, located in Berkeley, California, on the rim of the Pacific basin, we have a good many students in our classes from other lands and especially from Asia. I (RCL) recall having a Korean student who always sat on the front row in my class and who listened to every word with unusual intentness. He had a very expressive face. Every now and then as I was lecturing, I would become aware of a blank expression that would cross his face. I would know then that I had used some colloquial expression in an American context which the English-language courses in his homeland had not included. Obviously no communication was taking place, and some alternative form of expression was needed.

Harry Stack Sullivan was an expert at hearing the unspoken message behind the spoken word. He notes that prejudiced positions may rarely be attacked directly because they are protection against great anxiety.

These flaming convictions are experienced as indispensably useful; one would be much less of a person if one were to relinquish them or open them to an assessment of their relative rather than absolute importance. In other words, these never-to-be-yielded convictions and never-to-be-compromised positions—and along with them sundry never-to-be-questioned prejudices—are functioning as *effective protection* against great anxiety.[9]

Like Harry Stack Sullivan, Elisabeth Kübler-Ross developed extraordinary capacity to communicate in more-than-verbal ways. She tells of the special language that is needed to communicate with those who are dying. When an eight-year-old girl, who was dying of leukemia and was being treated in an oxygen tent, asked her nurse, "What's going to happen when I'm inside the oxygen tent and fire breaks out?" she was really asking to talk about dying. Understanding the unspoken question, the nurse unzipped the oxygen tent, put her arms around the little girl, held her tightly, and then asked, "Does this help?" The little girl's response was to begin to cry and then to say: "I know I'm going to die very soon and just have to talk to somebody about it."[10]

It is significant that language was the gift from the Holy Spirit. Language was the gift needed to empower the disciples with the tool they needed to spread the "mighty works of God" to the far corners of the ancient world. The writer is saying that God provided the one thing needed to spread the new faith. Here was the beginning of the missionary movement of Christianity.

Releasing power

The Pentecost experience provided a releasing of power for the disciples, but left the multitude "amazed and perplexed" (2:12). Their reaction was one of bewilderment and wonder (2:6, 7) and led them to ask: "What does this mean?" (2:12).

Here again we are confronted with the distinction between the telling of history and the symbolic expression of a religious truth. Those who wanted to understand the event in a historical sense found an explanation only in mockery: "They are filled with new wine" (2:13). But those who were willing to see the event through the eyes of faith found, with Peter's help,[11] the fulfillment of Old Testament promises (2:16-21).

Thornton Wilder has a vivid passage in which he deals with the problem that contemporary people have with miracles. He puts these words in the mouth of an articulate but down-to-earth landlady, Mrs. Wickersham: "I don't believe in miracles, but I couldn't exist if I didn't feel that things like miracles were happening all around me. Of course, there's an explanation for what you've told me—but explanations are for people who carry dull minds through dull lives."[12]

The multitudes were like Mrs. Wickersham's people "who carry dull minds through dull lives." They were puzzled by what they saw, but they were not prompted to do anything about it. No power was released in their lives because they looked only at superficialities and ignored the deeper issues. They only saw the disciples as drunk and had no concept of the transforming power of a new way of living. James Ashbrook speaks of Pentecost as providing a glimpse of a new reality to those whose eyes are open.

> Pentecost provides a glimpse of New Reality. Rather than explaining community, it describes community. We think and we speak in the divine tongue, that is, with the gift of standing-under each other's experienced world. We are apart from *and* we are part of the divine community, that is, present to one another. . . . The Pentecostal task demands that we exegete, translate, and interpret every surface tongue as transformation of deep structure. . . . New Reality discloses cross-cultural imperative.[13]

The disciples *did* glimpse the new reality. The Spirit-descent promised since Luke 3:16 (baptism with Spirit and fire) results in the disciples in the release of subconscious dynamics (the prophesying, the seeing of visions, the dreaming of dreams) accompanied by external signs (the showing forth of "wonders in the heavens above and signs on the earth beneath" (2:19). Both the invisible heavens and the visible earth are affected.

For the disciples the language barrier—the barrier that halts communication across cultures—melts away. What had been impossible or required extraordinary human effort now becomes spontaneous.

Becoming transformed

The fourth issue of concern to us in this passage is the promise of transformation. Indeed, the disciples were transformed. Mary Ellen Chase uses the picturesque imagery of the Book of Revelation to describe transformation on earth as well as in the heavens:

> There were nights of northern lights streaming across the sky like the expanding wings of the seraphim, piercing the clouds with radiance, dimming the stars. With these it was impossible not to see the wind as companion, even as master, the power behind those shooting, soaring paths of flame, clearing the way . . . for the streets of the New Jerusalem, blazing with topaz and emerald.[14]

For the disciples the transformation, clearing the way for them for the New Jerusalem, was from a dejected and despairing group to bold and courageous missionaries. Acts 4:31 characterizes the change: ". . . the place in which they were gathered together was shaken; and they were all filled with the Holy Spirit and spoke the word of God with boldness."[15] When the author of Acts (i.e., Luke) brings in the prophecy from Joel, he introduces an ominous and threatening note: "The sun shall be turned into darkness and the moon into blood" (2:20). It is as if Luke is saying that there can be no transformation until the threatening element has been dealt with. Indeed, we have met this idea many times before. It is when potentially destructive forces are harnessed and channeled that wondrous things are accomplished. In Joel's prophecy[16] the promised and threatened total transformation (2:19-20) will be a "saving" one for those who call on the name of the Lord, i.e., those who remain open to the source of transformation.

To remain open to the transforming influence of God is the secret of many who have sensed a power operating in themselves that is not of their own making. James Muilenberg, Old Testament scholar, writes of his own experience:

> In looking over my past experience, I cannot resist the conviction that it has not been primarily my seeking and searching that has been important, but rather the awareness of *being sought and found* by Another. . . . In my best moments it is most natural to think of a Living God who has "invaded" the chaos and confusion of life to give it strength and vitality and hope.[17]

And "strength and vitality and hope" are needed, because any transformation by the Spirit of God calls for witness in the presence of injustice, for coming to terms with "signs on the earth beneath, blood, and fire, and vapor of smoke," (2:19). Viktor Frankl writes of the responsibility that the religious person feels: "The religious man . . . interprets his existence not only in terms of being responsible *for* fulfilling his life tasks, but also as being responsible *to* the taskmaster."[18]

As always, the joy and gladness so often associated with the Holy Spirit is in tension with the blood and fire of human suffering. It is the Holy Spirit that directs sensitive souls from a vision of the heavens to do battle with the forces of evil on earth.

> The Spirit of the Lord God is upon me,
>   because the Lord has anointed me
> to bring good tidings to the afflicted;
>   he has sent me to bind up the brokenhearted,
> to proclaim liberty to the captives,
>   and the opening of the prison to those who are bound;
> To proclaim the year of the Lord's favor. (Isaiah 61:1-2*a*)

Chapter Eleven / Laughing

[II CORINTHIANS 11:21b–12:10]

FOR THE MOST PART, the New Testament is a pretty serious book. There are occasional light moments, however, and the passage in II Corinthians 11:21b to 12:10 is one of them. In a surprising way, Paul's words are to be read as dancing with humor.[1] When he writes, "I am speaking as a fool" (11:21b), he is writing with a light touch. Earlier he put it very clearly: "I wish you would bear with me in a little foolishness" (11:1).[2]

Paul is quite willing to be a fool[3] "for Christ's sake" (I Cor. 4:10). The whole Christian story with the cross as its central symbol is foolishness to the uninitiated, but to the followers of Christ it speaks of the power of God. In Paul's earlier letter to the Corinthians he wrote: "The word of the cross is folly to those who are perishing, but to us who are being saved it is the power of God" (I Cor. 1:18). Here is a reminder of how surprisingly different the Christian way is from the way of the world.

Thornton Wilder, in his novel *The Eighth Day,* writes of this difference between God's way and the perspective of most people. "The sign of God's way is that it is strange. God is strange. There is nothing more childish than to think of God as a man."[4] The novel is a plea to look deeper into life, to see below the surface into deeper meanings, to learn to look at life through God's eyes and thus see a world in which strange and unexpected things can happen. The novel begins with a strange, almost impossible event:

97

Your father fired a rifle; a man near him fell dead, but your father did not kill the man. That is strange. Your father did not lift a finger to save himself, but he was saved. That is strange. Your father had no friends, he says; but friends saved him. Your mother never left her house; she had no money; she was dazed. But a child who had never held a dollar in his hand sustained a house. Is that not strange?[5]

Wilder goes on to talk about the ordinary people who made up the family tree of Jesus.

There are some names here of whom the Bible tells us discreditable things. Is that not strange? You and I would say in our ignorance that the men and women who were so near to bearing a Messiah would be pure and without fault, but no! God builds in His own way. He can use the stone that the builders rejected. There is an old saying, "God moves in a mysterious way his wonders to perform."[6]

There are three issues in this passage that we want to lift up.

Experiencing power unexpectedly

It is Paul's surprising affirmation that strength is found in those moments when he feels weak: "I am content with weaknesses, insults, hardships, persecutions, and calamities; for when I am weak, then I am strong" (12:10b). But his secret is that he sees those moments of apparent weakness as opportunities. These are times when Christ can work in him ("for the sake of Christ," 12:10a).

Here is an affirmation that things may not be as negative as they seem. Things do work out! When Paul mentions his escape from Damascus, undignified as it was, he is affirming the way that things unexpectedly work out. Here is a reaffirmation of his familiar words: "We know that in everything God works for good with those who love him, who are called according to his purpose" (Rom. 8:28).[7]

A contemporary expression of this assertion is found in the attitude of a college student in East Germany who was awarded a Crusade Scholarship by the American Methodist church. When the East German government refused to issue her a permit to leave home to travel to America, she decided to go anyway. Heavily bundled for the winter in an old army coat, she made her way to the exit point at a remote frontier station and joined the line of travelers who were being processed slowly through the checkpoint. Having no exit permit, her anxiety mounted as she moved closer and closer to the barrier. Then she noticed that footprints in the snow made a path to a latrine some hundred yards or so away from the gate, situated right on the border fence. She noted, too, that a second path went from the other side of the latrine to the West German side of the barrier. Apparently in that rather remote checkpoint station, the same latrine was used by officials on both sides of the barrier. When she was sure that no one was using the latrine, she mustered her courage and walked unobtrusively up the path to the latrine, went inside, stayed briefly, went out the other side, and walked down the path to mingle with people on the West German side in freedom! Her faith that things would work out for her was so strong that she did the impossible. Talking later with friends in America, she declared: "It seemed to me that coming to America was what God wanted me to do."

In an unexpected way, suffering can lead to strength and hence can be welcomed. To be sure, suffering is not always an occasion for growth. Indeed, for most people suffering is an issue to be avoided. If one grows toward alienation from self (or resignation from life), then suffering becomes a liability. This liability shows up in our text on two sides: (a) the Corinthian congregation who began to call into question the integrity and authenticity of Paul's standing as Apostle (see II Corinthians, chapters 1–7); and (b) Paul himself who, like Jesus in Gethsemane, asked for the cup of suffering to be taken from him (II Cor. 12:7-9).

The temptation to give up the struggle for growth is vividly described in William Gibson's play *The Miracle Worker*. The play tells the true story of how little Helen

Keller, a six-year-old child who was blind and deaf and hence dumb, was taught to speak by her teacher, Annie Sullivan. At one point Annie confronts Helen's parents:

Annie:	Mrs. Keller, I don't think Helen's worst handicap is deafness or blindness. I think it's your love. And pity.
Keller:	Now what does that mean?
Annie:	All of you here are so sorry for her you've kept her—like a pet, why, even a dog you housebreak. No wonder she won't let me come near her. It's useless for me to try to teach her language or anything else here.[8]

In the script originally prepared for a television broadcast, this last speech is amplified a bit:

Annie:	All of you are so sorry for her you've kept her from becoming a human being. . . . I think what makes a human being is choosing, Mrs. Keller. You've always given Helen the easy thing, she doesn't know what choice is. She won't come near *me* for days now.[9]

In a similar way Annie challenges Keller to choose to support her in her efforts at training Helen, even when trouble and pain are involved.[10]

The theme of choice emphasized in these lines is also a dominant theme in Paul's "fool's speech." He is presenting a choice to the Corinthians. Either they can follow the "superlative apostles" (11:5), who cause deception by offering "another Jesus" and a "different spirit" and a "different gospel" (11:4), or they can follow Paul. The temptation to go the easy way is constantly present and may appear in different disguises at different times in a person's life.[11]

Suffering can become an asset. It becomes an asset when it is used as a means toward self-integration. This asset shows up on two sides: (a) the Macedonian churches stood by Paul when, despite a "severe test of affliction" on their part, they worked with Paul for the collection for the saints in Jerusalem (II Corinthians, chapters 8–9); and (b) Paul himself who, as servant of Christ, boasts of his weakness (11:23-29; 11:30; 12:5 and 12:10).

Laughing

Experiencing weakness unexpectedly

While it is true that power may be experienced unexpectedly, it is also true that weakness may be experienced when least expected. Paul tells of experiencing "visions and revelations" (12:1),[12] but then goes on to describe a "thorn . . . in the flesh" that harassed him in his euphoria.

C. G. Jung writes that Paul was "one of those people whose unconscious was disturbed and produced revelatory ecstasies."[13] Such "revelatory ecstasies" turn out to be far more common than many of us have been led to believe. In Frank Barron's studies of creativity at the University of California, he discovered that truly creative people seem to be able to expand the ordinary limits of consciousness in a way that often is spoken of as illness. Barron notes, however, that the creative persons studied were "outstandingly sane men":

> The expansion of consciousness requires the temporary abandonment of certain ego structures, at least the crustier outside ones which are farthest from the core of what William James called "the transcendental ego" (which I conceive of as "inside" or "within" in the same sense in which Christ spoke of the kingdom of God as "within").[14]

> Paranoia bears a puzzling relationship to certain intense experiences of a religious, transcendental, or mystical nature, whose existence we know best from the reports of outstandingly sane men. [In paranoia there is a] relinquishing of the experience of boundedness and separateness of subject from object.[15]

Barron goes on to note how many truly creative persons (writers, in this case) report having had mystical experiences in the sense of feeling a sense of unity with the universe:

> Nearly 40 percent of the group of representative successful writers reported having had such experiences, and over 50 percent of the specially selected group of creative writers reported similar experiences.[16]

101

Expanding the usual boundaries of consciousness is one of the marks of a creative person. In this sense Paul takes his place along with the saints who, in some often misunderstood way, saw more deeply into the heart of the world than most of us are inclined to see.

Even as Paul saw deeper than most, even as he was rejoicing in his visions, he was kept "from being too elated" by a "thorn . . . in the flesh" (12:7). It is not clear what Paul's thorn in the flesh[17] was, but it is clear that the discomfort which he tried so hard to get rid of eventually became a means for growth. C. G. Jung writes of how necessary suffering is for growth: "To round itself out, life calls not for perfection but for completeness; and for this the 'thorn in the flesh' is needed, the suffering of defects without which there is no progress and no ascent."[18]

Paul's experience, as underscored by Jung, is a common one. What seems to be a barrier often turns out to be a means of growth. Viktor Frankl sees suffering, when it is unavoidable, as a potent way of finding meaning in life.

Frankl knows about suffering. During World War II he spent two and a half years as a prisoner in four different concentration camps, including Auschwitz and Dachau. His personal history validates his conviction that a person's life is determined not by the circumstances to which he or she is exposed but by the responses he or she makes. The attitude that one takes toward what life has brought can make for meaning even in the most impossible circumstances. Frankl cites a woman who had periodically recurring depressions which did not respond to usual medication. He tells how he worked with her.

> Here was a case where logotherapeutic treatment was necessary. It was the doctor's business to show the patient that her very affliction—these fated . . . recurrent depressions—posed a challenge for her. Since men are free to take a rational position on psychic processes, she was free to take a positive attitude toward it—or, in other words, to the actualization of what we have called attitudinal values. In time the patient learned to see her life as full of personal

tasks, in spite of her states of dejection. Moreover, she learned to consider these states as presenting one more task: the task of somehow getting along with them and being superior to them. After this existential analysis—for that was what it was—she was able, in spite of and even during further phases of endogenous [i.e., organically determined] depression, to lead a life that was more conscious of responsibility and more filled with meaning than before treatment—more so, probably, than if she had never fallen ill and never needed treatment. One day this patient was able to write to her doctor: "I was not a human being until you made me one."[19]

Coping through laughter

It is the paradox of the Christian faith that "power is made perfect in weakness" (12:9). As in the case of Frankl's patient who found a new dimension of being human through her suffering, power comes in unexpected ways. Often the key to finding strength even in weakness lies in laughter.[20]

Norman Cousins, for many years the distinguished editor of *Saturday Review,* gives an autobiographical account of how, through humor, he conquered an illness that appeared to be incurable. Confronted by a disease of the connective tissues that completely incapacitated him, and told by his doctors that he had only one chance in five hundred for a full recovery, he set about to demonstrate his long-held conviction that "the positive emotions are life-giving experiences."[21] He argued with his doctor, "If negative emotions produce negative chemical changes in the body, wouldn't the positive emotions produce positive chemical changes?"[22] Viewing comical films of Allen Funt's popular television series *Candid Camera* and old Marx Brothers films, he "made the joyous discovery that ten minutes of genuine belly laughter had an anesthetic effect and would give . . . at least two hours of painfree sleep."[23] Laughter turned out to be a good medicine and, combined with massive doses of ascorbic acid (vitamin C), led to his virtual complete recovery.

Viktor Frankl describes how he used humor in treating a deeply depressed woman who was plagued with an obsession about germs. He said to her: "You need not fight your obsessive ideas. You may as well joke with them."[24] Paradoxically he invited her to intend the very thing she feared. Having her kneel beside him on the floor of the clinic lecture hall, he had her follow his example of rubbing his hands on the floor, then rubbing his face. He tells his procedure in his own words: "Stooping and rubbing my hands on the floor, I continued: 'See, I cannot get dirty enough; I can't find enough bacteria.' "[25] He tells of the results:

> Under my encouragement the patient followed my example. And so she began the treatment which, in five days, removed ninety percent of her symptoms. . . . Thus an incapacitating pattern of three years' standing was broken up in a matter of a few weeks. She spoke jokingly of all her former symptoms. She asked her fellow patients whether any of them could provide her with "some more bacteria."[26]

Frank Barron, referring to the creative process, tells how looking back one can laugh at apparently impossible obstacles.

> Looking backwards from the end point of the creative process, we are inclined to say, "Ah, yes, it had to be so; the chance had to be taken; the chalice could not be passed; the agony was necessary for the redemption and the resurrection." But facing forward in time we see only risk and difficulty, and if we have not the courage to endure diffusion ("suffer death") we cannot achieve the new and more inclusive integration ("gain the light").[27]

The gospel record is very clear: though poor, we are rich; though strong, we are weak. The paradox that makes us fools for Christ calls for us to hang in there in "weaknesses, insults, hardships, persecutions, and calamities" (12:10), laughing off both unexpected strength and unexpected weakness, knowing that God's "grace is sufficient" (12:9).

CHAPTER TWELVE / LISTENING

[LUKE 10:38-42]

A PART OF THE APPEAL of the Christian faith is the unexpectedness of its challenge. Again and again in the New Testament record, in the midst of an apparently innocuous incident, a call to a radical commitment suddenly appears. Such is the case in the conversation that Jesus had with the sisters Martha and Mary in their home in Bethany.

The story here develops quite naturally. Jesus has turned aside from his disciples to renew his friendship with Mary and Martha, perhaps as a brief respite from his teaching and training of his disciples. The two sisters entertain him in the usual pattern of Near East hospitality: Martha preparing a meal for his refreshment, and Mary attentive to his conversation. It is only when Martha complains to Jesus that Mary isn't helping her and asks him to admonish Mary that Jesus participates in the interaction.

It is the way in which Jesus participates that provides the surprise in this incident. Instead of criticizing Mary, as Martha had requested, he criticizes Martha for her attitude. And the record indicates that he did it with intensity, calling her name twice. His concluding words (pronouncement[1]) point up the contrast between "many things" that one can be anxious about and the "one thing" that is needful.[2] The pronouncement focuses first on Martha's anxious busyness and then on Mary's "better part." Both parts of the comment accent the same message: many things are useful and important, but only one thing is of ultimate importance. Martha is criticized not because what she is doing is wrong or even unimportant but because it blinds her to a more important need. In the very act of doing a kindly task for Jesus she overlooks a deeper need on his part. In her preoccupation with getting a meal, she ignores the special need that he has for someone to listen to him in a concerned and uninterrupted way. Her anxiety about making adequate preparation for a very special guest was quite understandable, but when it got in the way of meeting some of Jesus' other needs, it became a problem.

One of the common tragedies of everyday life is played out whenever urgent personal needs are overlooked as routine life is carried on. Martin Buber tells in graphic terms of an occasion when a young man with deep personal needs sought him out, but did not reveal how distressed he was. Preoccupied with routine concerns, Buber missed the hints of distress, only to discover that the young man subsequently committed suicide. He writes sadly of the experience:

> I conversed attentively and openly with him—only I omitted to guess the questions which he did not put. Later, not long after, I learned from one of his friends—he himself was no longer alive—the essential content of these questions; I learned that he had come to see me not casually, but borne by destiny, not for a chat but for a decision. He had come to me, he had come in this hour.[3]

Arthur Miller writes of a similar failure to meet urgent human need in a dialogue between Willy and Linda in *Death of a Salesman*. Willy, the salesman, is trying to tell his wife of the awful sense of failure he is experiencing, and Linda responds only in terms of taking an aspirin:

Willy: *(after a pause)* I suddenly couldn't drive any more. The car kept going off on the shoulder, y'know?

Linda: *(helpfully)* Oh. Maybe it was the steering again. . . .

Willy: No, it's me, it's me. Suddenly I realize I'm goin' sixty miles an hour and I don't remember the last five minutes. I'm—I can't seem to—keep my mind to it.

Linda: Maybe it's your glasses. . . .

Willy: No. I see everything. I came back ten miles an hour. It took me nearly four hours from Yonkers.

Linda: *(resigned)* Well, you'll just have to take a rest. . . . Take an aspirin. Should I get you an aspirin? It'll soothe you.[4]

The same failure to sense an urgent personal need is found in Martha as her concern for hospitality blinds her to needs at a much deeper level.

It is of considerable interest that the Martha and Mary incident immediately follows the story of the good Samaritan (Luke 10:29-37). It is as if the editor of Luke's Gospel chose to put these two incidents one after the other in order to accent the complete gospel. The good Samaritan story underscores serving. The Martha and Mary story stresses listening. Neither is unimportant, but the "one thing" that Mary did (the listening) is the more important. It is hard for some people to see Jesus as a person who had very human needs. That he could sometimes be tired and impatient and cross is hard to accept, and that he could be angry is even harder to realize, but the record is very clear. He had his moments, just as all of us do, when his own needs momentarily overrode his sense of mission. We believe the brief stay with Martha and Mary in Bethany could be taken as one of those moments.

The Martha and Mary story is one of the numerous "plotted incidents" in Luke.[5] The plotting is patterned after Israel's wilderness journey, which shows Israel in the service of God but distracted from doing what is needful. In the good Samaritan story, the priest and the Levite were preoccupied with "serving" (filling "roles") even after their assigned service was completed, for both were on their way home ("going down that road").

Sharing both the positive and the negative

There are several issues we would like to point to in this passage. The first is the statement with which the Lukan travel[6] section begins, that Jesus "set his face to go to Jerusalem" (9:51). When Luke 10:38 reads "as they went on their way," the "on their way" refers to the movement toward Jerusalem which began in 9:51.[7] The King James Version makes this beginning even more emphatic: "He steadfastly set his face to go to Jerusalem." It is in this section, as Jesus and his disciples were "on their way" toward Jerusalem, that much of the instruction to the disciples took place.[8]

Facing Jerusalem had both positive and negative elements for Jesus. On the positive side, he was going home to the Father.[9] He had just come from a literal mountaintop experience where he had sensed his continuity with Moses and Elijah (9:28-36), each well known for his own distinctive exodus. There was a joy to be shared in his sense of participating in the ongoing history of fulfilling God's purposes. In Martha and Mary's home, likely the one-room house of that day (similar to early pioneer homes in our country), both sisters would overhear all that was being said and could share in his joy.

Personal sharing, at a significant level, involves the good as well as the bad. In our culture today, it is often easier to share the negative than the positive. We speak more quickly of the problems in everyday life than we do of the joys, and thereby lose opportunities to deepen the bonds of intimacy. One of the great values of anniversary occasions is that they encourage the sharing of positive feelings.

With Martha and Mary, however, the feelings of joy were overshadowed by the negative awareness Jesus had of conflict ahead. All of the events in the movement toward Jerusalem, including the Martha and Mary story, were colored by the inevitability of conflict with the authorities in Jerusalem. The record is very clear that Jesus knew what lay ahead. Many times he made references to his disciples about his impending death.[10] But on no occasion were they able to deal with it. Indeed, they refused to even listen to his talk about leaving them. With one exception, there was no one with whom he could talk about dying. That exception was Mary. It seems clear to us that when Mary sat at the feet of Jesus and "listened to his teaching," she was listening to him as he thought out loud about the life-and-death events ahead in Jerusalem. This was no casual conversation!

Facing impending death

Mary's willingness to face the facts of Jesus' impending death is the second issue we are interested in. The clue to understanding Mary at this point is found not in Luke but in John's Gospel (John 12:1-8).[11] John reports that six days before the Passover, Jesus was in the home of Martha and Mary (and Lazarus) in Bethany. In her usual role, Martha was serving. During the meal, Mary anointed the feet of Jesus with a costly ointment of pure nard and wiped his feet with her hair. When Judas, who was present, objected to the waste of the precious ointment, Jesus said: "Let her alone, let her keep it for the day of my burial." In Mark's Gospel, in a somewhat parallel passage, Jesus is recorded as having said: "She has done what she could; she has anointed my body beforehand for burying" (Mark 14:8, Matt. 26:12).

From this passage it seems clear that Mary acknowledged Jesus' own awareness that he must die. No one other than Mary had been willing even to entertain a thought about his impending death. Moses and Elijah had done their share on the mountain, and later in Gethsemane an angel would be doing that service.

This incident is more about Mary and about Jesus than it is about Martha. It is about Mary's sensitivity to Jesus' urgent need to be able to talk with someone about what lay ahead. When Mary "sat[12] at the Lord's feet and listened to his teaching" there is an appropriateness that is underscored by our best understanding of the needs of persons in crisis. In a crisis situation, the need is not for advice but for someone to listen, not for direction but for someone to whom fears of the unknown can be expressed. One of the most significant findings from research in ministry in crisis is that the real need is for support in facing openly whatever the facts may be. The help needed is not so much professional guidance as it is concerned presence. Simply to be present in a concerned and involved way makes a significant contribution that might mean the difference between coping and failure.

Everyone knows the experience of wanting to be alone with someone where all defenses can be put aside, where all barriers can be let down. What Jesus needed was not disciples to dispute with him about his future but a friend to whom he could pour out his soul and get a concerned, sympathetic hearing.

Mary's role is all the more unusual when we think of the place that women characteristically held in the Jewish culture of that day. Women's work was to "serve."[13] They were not expected to "study" like disciples. It was almost unheard of that a woman would be sought out as a confidante or that a man would discuss with a woman matters of life and death. That Jesus singled out Mary is an indication of how far his attitudes veered from the typical masculine orientation of his day.[14]

We have been saying that the "one thing needful" was a personal concern for Jesus and what he was going through. Jesus' teaching, to which Mary listened, was about God and God's claim on a person's life. This was consistently what Jesus talked about and acted out. With this in mind, it is more important to listen to Jesus' teaching than it is to be concerned about preparing a meal.

Choosing follows listening

The third issue is the implication that listening to the word involves making a choice about keeping it. In Luke 11:28, Jesus is very explicit: "Blessed . . . are those who hear the word of God and keep it." The listening posture is not a momentary thing but one to be cultivated constantly. When Jesus said of Mary that she had "chosen the good portion" (10:42), he was underscoring the power of the person to make a choice. By implication he was saying to Martha that she had made a choice too.[15]

The disciples are barely mentioned in this story (see the opening sentence: "Now as they went on their way"), but the difference between Mary who listened and Martha who did not has implications for the disciples, and, indeed, for all of us. As a group, the disciples were not very good at sitting down and taking in. They were more like Martha than like Mary. They were preoccupied with their own concerns and so were unresponsive to some of Jesus' needs.[16] At the Garden of Gethsemane, while Jesus agonized over the decisions he needed to make, his disciples slept (22:45).

Saving face

The fourth issue accents the culture in which Martha lived. Instead of confronting Mary directly, Martha tried to work through Jesus. The immediate reaction of most of us in the Western world is to ask why Martha didn't go directly to Mary. Why was it necessary to go to Jesus at all? But the ways of the Eastern world follow precisely the route that Martha took. Instead of open and direct confrontation, the Eastern world characteristically works through a third person to avoid any loss of face on anyone's part. Martha's approach to Jesus was thoroughly consistent with the culture in which she lived.

It is of interest that Martha felt free to place her complaints before Jesus. Implied here is a relationship of trust and openness. She even dared to tell him what to do!

It is notable that Jesus did not do what Martha asked him to do. Like any good counselor, he decided what was appropriate and followed his own decision rather than simply acquiescing to what was asked of him. Effective counselors cannot do whatever the counselee asks and maintain any kind of professional integrity. Counselors need to believe that their perception of reality is at least as accurate as that of other persons, and that their perception is probably better than that of the person making a request. Indeed, the emotional distance that counselors establish protects against personal bias colored by emotional entanglements.

What Jesus did do was to try to teach Martha about ultimate concerns. Like any good teacher, he waited until a "teachable moment"—until that moment when Martha raised the issue herself. We have no way of knowing how effective the teaching may have been, but we do know that until Martha's own feelings had been looked at, there was little hope of her making any change in her life. Jesus tried to help Martha understand that her preoccupation with little things made any recognition of really important things, and indeed of the most important thing, virtually impossible.

Theologian Paul Tillich, in a sermon entitled "Our Ultimate Concern,"[17] writes of the importance that he attaches to this story: "The words Jesus speaks to Martha belong to the *most famous* of all words in the Bible."[18] It is not enough to have meaning in one's life; it is crucial that the meaning one seeks is the ultimate concern.

CHAPTER THIRTEEN / INTEGRATING

[EPHESIANS 4:7-16]

A FEW VERSES IN the letter to the church at Ephesus bring together in a remarkable and quite unexpected way one of the most profound teachings of the Christian faith. This is the scandalous assertion that in Christ God descended to the human level of life and lived, momentarily, among people.[1] For Jews and Greeks alike, this was truly a scandalous concept. For any "commonsense" person, it doesn't make any sense at all.

Some of the major problems in religious thinking grow out of a confusion of what the religious dimension in life really is. If the Bible is read only as a statement of historic fact, with commonsense explanations and without ambiguities, then much of its significance is lost. Like any significant religious literature, the Bible deals more in symbols than in signs, more in myths than in facts. When C. G. Jung speaks of a "boundless expanse full of unprecedented uncertainty,"[2] he is providing a good definition of much religious writing. Indeed, it is Jung who, among psychologists, helps us the most in shifting from a "subjective and personalistic, essentially *biographical* approach . . . to a larger culture-historical, *mythological* orientation."[3]

Paul Tillich, eminent theologian of our century, describes how incomprehensible this issue is if read in nonmythic ways:

> If the symbols of the Savior and salvation through Him which point to the healing power in history and personal life

113

are transferred to the horizontal plane, they become stories of a half-divine being coming from a heavenly place and returning to it. Obviously, in this form, they have no meaning whatsoever for people, whose view of the universe is determined by scientific astronomy.[4]

This passage deals with the uniqueness of the gifts with which each person is endowed. It is written against a special internal problem in the newly developing Christian church: the later "intolerance" of Gentile Christianity replaces the former "intolerance" of Jewish Christianity, a racism of sorts in either case. There are three aspects of this problem we want to discuss.

Finding unity in diversity

The main thrust of this passage is the assertion that unity comes best through the recognition of diversity. Real unity does not mean the elimination of diversity. Rather, it means welcoming the uniqueness of the many parts so that the final unity is more complete.

Ephesians 4:7-16 is similar to I Corinthians 12, in which Paul argued for the effectiveness of a unity that grows out of the encouragement of diversity in order that individual and unique gifts may contribute to the whole. In memorable words in I Corinthians 12, and with a bit of refreshing humor, Paul describes how individual parts of a human body are indispensable for the effective working of the whole body, and then designates individual persons as members of the body of Christ. He does this with a humorous note which is characteristic of many of his writings.

The specific problem in the early church at Ephesus is a constantly recurring problem in any age. In our own day, the Moral Majority seeks a uniformity which virtually denies individual opinion and calls for a sameness in point of view which is sharply contrary to this passage. Now, as then, some believe that there is only one way, and that any deviation from the one way (defined by them as *the* right way) is unacceptable. In contrast, we are reminded of the power in diversity provided that the diversity supports "one Lord, one faith, one baptism, one God and Father of us all" (4:5).

The issue of unity through diversity is very present today in ethnic communities, where the "melting pot" ideal is giving way to a "salad bowl" approach. Rather than asking each ethnic group to lose its uniqueness through a melding into a generalized uniformity, the goal now is to accent uniqueness in order that the resulting whole may be richer and "tastier." It is the diversified nature of the parts that enriches the whole.

In James Michener's *Hawaii,* there is a vivid illustration of this kind of diversity. There was a tense moment in the production of pineapples in the Hawaiian Islands when suddenly and without warning the pineapple plants throughout the islands began to die. Recognizing that some chemical deficiency in the soil was probably responsible, a spray was developed which included every known chemical component which might possibly be lacking. When the spray was used on the dying plants, they came back to life in a dramatic recovery. By withholding first one chemical and then another, it was finally determined which chemical was adding the needed ingredient. The red soil of Hawaii was thus perceived as a bank from which supplies needed to be replaced when withdrawn. Hoxworth Hale, one of the chief plantation owners, then had a vision of Hawaii as a great pineapple field: "No man could say out of hand what contribution the Filipino or the Korean or the Norwegian had made, but if anyone stole from Hawaii those things which the tiniest component added to the society, perhaps the human pineapples would begin to perish."[5]

One of the significant developments in the counseling world is the recognition of the insights available from many diversified sources. Whether it is the medicine man of Africa or the native healer of Malaysia or the unlettered storefront preacher, a good deal of intuitive wisdom is discovered in nonprofessional counselors as they deal with perennial human problems. Western counseling methods, largely limited in usefulness to upper-middle-class white society, are being complemented by age-old approaches that draw more on common sense than on technical professional training. There is no single counseling approach to human need.

Maya Angelou, the black author, tells of a time when, in deep despair, she sought help from a white psychiatrist. He asked her: "Are you troubled?" She describes her feelings:

> Yes, I was troubled; why else would I be here? But could I tell this man? Would he understand Arkansas, which I left, yet would never, could never leave? Would he comprehend why my brilliant brother, who was the genius in our family, was doing time in Sing Sing on a charge of fencing stolen goods instead of sitting with clean fingernails in a tailor-made suit, listening to some poor mad person cry her blues out? How would he perceive a mother who, in a desperate thrust for freedom, left her only child who became sick during her absence? A mother who, upon her return, felt so guilty she could think of nothing more productive than killing herself and possibly even the child? . . . No, I couldn't tell him about living inside a skin that was hated or feared by the majority of one's fellow citizens or about the sensation of getting on a bus on a lovely morning, feeling happy, and suddenly seeing the passengers curl their lips in distaste or avert their eyes in revulsion. No, I had nothing to say to the doctor.[6]

Maya Angelou left the white psychiatrist abruptly and sought out "Uncle" Wilkie, an old friend, a singing teacher who was black. His approach was in sharp contrast to the white psychiatrist. He held her in a warm embrace, gave her a stiff drink, and then sat her down at his desk and had her write down what she had to be thankful for. He started her off with the fact that she was able to hear what he told her to do, and that she could speak well enough to have directed the taxi to his studio. After she had completed her list and had discovered how much she really had going for herself, he sent her to a theatrical agency to apply for a job. Walking to the door with his arm around her, he said, "Let Uncle

Wilkie tell you one last thing. Don't ask God to forgive you, for that's already done. Forgive yourself."[7]

Integrating the shadow

If unity is to be found in diversity, the diversity needs to be all-inclusive. The second issue in this passage centers in the need to integrate the best and the worst in a person's life. To ascend implies a descent.[8] To attain the heights implies a dealing with the depths.

Much of the therapeutic world is devoted to helping people accept all of themselves, not just the part that feels acceptable. Jung introduced the concept of the shadow to stand for "the dark or inferior personality composed of those elements which have been repressed because they would be too painful to be held in consciousness."[9] In order to attain any kind of maturity, Jung declared, the shadow aspect of life needs to be integrated into conscious life.

Fritz Kunkel, one of the earliest exponents of a marriage between psychology and Christianity, writes graphically of the shadow:

> Then Jesus says, "love your enemy," and Peter must forgive Judas. The reader must redeem his own inner enemy. The Shadow must be integrated or Christ, the center of the inner drama, will never come to life. Dynamic reading is the mobilization of all the conflicting forces in the reader's soul. Good and evil tendencies, high and low powers, selfish and unselfish goals must be contrasted, and manifested and reconciled. There is no forgiveness, no reconciliation, without our conscious recognition of the negative force that has to be cleansed and accepted.[10]

One way to make contact with the shadow, the parts of life that have been repressed, is through dreams. It is in dreams that we make the most direct contact with the mythological orientation referred to earlier. In Arthur Miller's *After the Fall*, Holga, who has lived through a concentration camp imprisonment in World War II, tells of a dream she had.

The same dream returned each night until I dared not go to
sleep and grew quite ill. I dreamed I had a child, and even in
the dream I saw it was my life, and it was an idiot, and I ran
away. But it always crept onto my lap again, clutched at my
clothes. Until I thought, if I could kiss it, whatever in it was
my own, perhaps I could sleep. And I bent to its broken face,
and it was horrible . . . but I kissed it.[11]

In the depths of her life was an experience which had to be
recognized and acknowledged and integrated into her being.
No matter how horrible it seemed, how impossible to accept, it
had to be brought into awareness and made a conscious part
of her being. Holga goes on to say to her lover, Quentin: "I
think one must finally take one's life in one's arms, Quentin."[12]
The implication is that one takes *all* of one's life.

This same image of the idiot child recurs later in the play.
The middle-aged lawyer Quentin is talking of how dangerous
each person is, how even murderous ideas are a part of each
person's life and need to be accepted and forgiven: "And the
wish to kill is never killed, but with some gift of courage one
may look into its face when it appears, and with a stroke of
love—as to an idiot in the home—forgive it; again and
again."[13]

One contemporary therapist declares that the basis of all
mental illness is the tendency to avoid suffering through
everyday problems.[14] C. G. Jung, as we have noted before, is
even more specific: "Neurosis is always a substitute for
legitimate suffering."[15] Jung describes the problem of
dealing with the shadow and the outcome:

The shadow is a tight pass, a narrow door, whose painful
constriction is spared to no one who climbs down into the
deep well-spring. But one must learn to know one-self in
order to know who one is. For what comes after the door is,
surprisingly enough, a boundless expanse full of unprecedented uncertainty.[16]

Achieving maturity

The final issue in Ephesians 4:7-16 deals with what it
means to be mature. A lack of maturity, that is, a failure to

have integrated all parts of one's being, leads to being like "babies . . . blown about and swung around by every wind of doctrine through the trickery of men with their ingenuity in inventing error" (4:14, Edgar J. Goodspeed, The Complete Bible: An American Translation, The University of Chicago Press. Copyright 1939 by the University of Chicago). This figure of speech is a vivid one for anyone who has observed boats swinging at anchor, changing position with each tide and with each new breeze.

On the positive side, maturity has three distinguishing qualities.[17] The first is the utilization of one's peculiar, indigenous gift for "building up the body of Christ." Maturity here is perceived in terms of contribution to community, of being involved not just on a personal journey but rather in a group enterprise.

The second quality of maturity is measured against "the stature of the fulness of Christ. . . . We are to grow up in every way into him who is the head." Whenever we want an example, we look to the life of Christ.

The third quality of maturity is found in a loving relationship in which the good of the whole takes priority over the development of the individual. The goal is not individual growth but the growth of the community, with each person "joined and knit together" with every other person to produce an effectively working whole.

To realize "speaking the truth in love" calls for a special kind of maturity. To love is not enough if love is perceived as always going along with whatever a loved person is doing. "Speaking the truth" by itself is not enough if in doing so injury is done to the other. But "speaking the truth in love" combines a loving attitude with a willingness to risk confrontation; it is a love which carries with it a sense of obligation to take exception to destructive patterns of behavior. It is a love which sometimes says no in the very interest of growth and effectiveness. It is a love character-ized by "patience" and "forbearing" (verse 2), but one which nevertheless does not hesitate to insist on growth.

It is not clear whether or not the writer of Ephesians[18] is writing about genuine integration. One scholar finds in much of Paul's writings in the New Testament a tendency toward further repression rather than a true integration of the shadow.[19] However this may be, "speaking the truth in love" suggests a direct confrontation of whatever is present when it is exercising a negative effect. The counseling world is pretty well in agreement that destructive patterns in interpersonal relationships need to be challenged. Nathan Ackerman is very clear on this point:

> For one human being professionally trained to help another one in distress, it is *sine qua non* that control of destructive interpersonal behavior be established. . . . The shunting of the goal of human relations away from love to purposes of power and destruction is the essence of perversion.[20]

When the most complete kind of integration is desired, then "speaking the truth in love" is needed.

CHAPTER FOURTEEN / NAMING

[REVELATION: 21:1–22:5]

WE HAVE BEEN SAYING that the New Testament is full of surprises. At no point is the surprise more evident than in the last book of the Bible. Revelation is full of surprises.

Revelation is not an easy book for modern people to read. Accustomed as we are to rational logic, to factual realism, to scientific order, we think this book makes little sense. But to a mind open to intuition rather than logic, to feelings rather than facts, to art rather than science, the book makes a lot of sense.

Revelation is written in the dimension of depth with access to the unconscious, and any attempts to reduce it to a world of historic fact or of future events miss its central thrust. The book is neither about Roman oppression or other external pressure nor about predictions of the future. Rather it describes an inner spiritual condition and gives an ideal picture of spiritual maturity in the form of a letter from Christ to seven Christian churches. In this sense the letter is very contemporary. It is not only the seven churches of Asia that struggle to find a renewed spiritual vitality in the presence of forces leading to disintegration![1]

There are three issues in Revelation 21:1–22:5[2] that we will discuss.

Releasing creativity

There is a dynamic quality to the passage, a stress on the releasing of creativity. We are dealing not with a static situation but with a dynamic process. It is a coming together of God on a throne in heaven and us, his people on earth. The coming together of heaven and earth, of husband (Lamb) and bride (holy city) is "new." This newness comprises Alpha and Omega, beginning and end (21:6).

This dynamic quality characterizes life itself. Research psychologist Frank Barron notes how the New Testament contrasts living flesh with inflexible law: "The New Testament is best understood in terms of the relationship between personified conscious knowledge—the Word made flesh, alive and changing, taking its chances, open to beauty and decay—and the ancient, rigid law and lawgiver, fixed, abstract, decided."[3]

In a similar vein psychologist Gordon Allport[4] entitles one of his books *Becoming* and makes a strong case for a psychological approach that pays attention to the dynamic quality of intentions, or goal orientations. His thesis is summarized in his critique of much psychological thinking, characterized by "a preference for externals rather than internals, for elements rather than patterns, for geneticism and for a passive or reactive organism rather than for one that is spontaneous and active."[5] He continues his critique by objecting to an aversion in most psychologists for "problems having to do with complex motives, high-level integration, with conscience, freedom, selfhood."[6]

One of the vivid illustrations used by Allport is that of Roald Amundsen, whose little Norwegian ship, the *Gjoa*, was on exhibit at Golden Gate Park in San Francisco for many years. Allport notes that Amundsen's life could never be understood apart from the goal of becoming an arctic explorer, which dominated his life from the age of fifteen.

> Having sailed the Northwest Passage, he embarked upon the painful project that led to the discovery of the South Pole. Having discovered the South Pole, he planned for years, against extreme discouragement, to fly over the North Pole, a task he finally accomplished. But his commitment never wavered until at the end he lost his life in attempting to rescue a less gifted explorer, Nobile, from death in the

Arctic. Not only did he maintain one style of life without ceasing, but this central commitment enabled him to withstand the temptation to reduce the segmental tensions continually engendered by fatigue, hunger, ridicule and danger.[7]

Viktor Frankl has always emphasized the need for a central commitment that unifies a personality and encourages creativity.

If you cannot grasp it intellectually, then you must believe in it emotionally. As long as I haven't found the supra-meaning but have only an inkling about it, I cannot wait until I am 80 years of age and only then dedicate myself to it, but must rely on my vague inkling and commit my heart in serving it. And this holds for God who is the warrant for the existence of supra-meaning, as mankind has developed the concept throughout history. Self-commitment and fulfillment of life's concrete challenge is the road at the end of which we are awaited by wisdom so that ultimate meaning becomes intelligible. This intellectual achievement is preceded by existential commitment. Trust in the wisdom of your heart, a wisdom which is deeper than the insight of your brain![8]

The secret of releasing creativity, however, comes in the source of power. Thornton Wilder underscores the source of that power: "All I ask is the chance to build new worlds and God has always given us that."[9] Here is the same affirmation as that given by the writer of Revelation: "God himself will be with them; he will wipe away every tear from their eyes, and death shall be no more, neither shall there be mourning nor crying nor pain any more, for the former things have passed away" (21:3-4).

Achieving identity

The second issue in this passage is the achieving of identity which is accomplished by the bringing together of polarities. The kings of the earth, who as recently as 19:19 were making war on the Word of God, are now bringing their glory into the glorious city. The very destructive and fornicating forces (the nations, the kings of the earth), which in the era of the "old heaven and old earth" provided much of the action provoking divine retribution, are now integrated. They "walk by its light" and "bring their glory into it" (21:24). Transformed are the qualities of the cowardly, faithless, polluted, murderers, fornicators, sorcerers, idolaters, all liars into earthly royal glories. Transformed are the traits of tears, mourning, crying, pain, and death (21:4, 8).

Moreover, dichotomies and barriers are removed. There is healing between the nation of Israel and the gentile nations. There is no day or night, no superior or inferior (22:2*b*-5).

The integration of opposites, which is one of the marks of spiritual maturity, turns out to be one of the characteristics of the most creative persons. Donald MacKinnon reported on an early stage of the research on creative persons which he and his associates carried out at the University of California at Berkeley by saying:

> If I were to summarize what at this stage of our researches most strikes me about the creative persons whom we have assessed, it is their openness to experience, and that they, more than most, are struggling with the opposites in their nature, striving ever for a more effective reconciliation of them, and seeking to tolerate and bind increasingly large quantities of tension as they strive for a creative solution to ever more difficult problems which are not set for them but which they set for themselves.[10]

Rather than eliminating opposites, creative persons find ways to encompass them in ways that make use of all that is, both positive and negative.

In recent times we have been hearing a good deal about the division in the brain between the right and left hemispheres. The left brain deals basically with rational processes, the kind of thinking that the Western scientific world is oriented to. The right brain, in contrast, deals with the intuitive side of life, the symbolic aspect that the Eastern world accents. This is the world of dynamic rather than static processes, of the depth dimension rather than the surface layers of life. It is in this depth dimension that John's Revelation is written.[11]

As we have indicated earlier, C. G. Jung, the Swiss psychiatrist, worked extensively with right brain processes. He tells of working with a woman whose life was plagued with neurotic problems. Of her he wrote: "I had to awaken mythological and religious ideas in her. . . . Thus her life took on meaning, and no trace of neurosis was left."[12] He sets forth his conviction clearly: "The more the critical reason dominates, the more impoverished life becomes; but the more of the unconscious, the more of myth we are capable of making conscious, the more of life we integrate."[13]

A more contemporary therapist, M. Scott Peck, tells of how he uses the unconscious to assist in therapy. He describes a patient.

> This man had started to work on a problem. Almost immediately his unconscious produced a drama that elucidated the cause of his problem, a cause of which he had previously been unaware. It did this through use of symbols in a manner as elegant as that of the most accomplished playwright. It is difficult to imagine that any other experience occurring at this point in his therapy could have been as eloquently edifying to him and me as this particular dream.[14]

The drama included a scene with the man's father in which his father was helping him find a boat on which he would take a journey. The father showed him a huge chest reaching to the ceiling with twenty or thirty enormous drawers. By sighting along the edge of the chest, the father told him, he could find the boat. When asked by Dr. Peck to talk about the chest, he said it reminded him of a sarcophagus or family vault with drawers big enough to hold a body, and then said, "Maybe I want to kill off my ancestors." Peck writes:

> The meaning of the dream was then clear. He had indeed in his youth been given a sight, a sighting for life, along the tombs of his famous dead paternal ancestors, and had been following this sighting toward fame. But he found it an oppressive force in his life and wished that he could psychologically kill off his ancestors so as to be free from this compulsive force.[15]

The bringing together of opposites has been a steady refrain throughout our book. A surprising aspect of the gospel is the way in which all parts of a personality, the bad as well as the good, are recognized and identified and integrated into a unified whole, a "new creation."

Claiming a name

In striking imagery, the writer of Revelation describes how God's name shall be written on people's foreheads (22:4). Identity is thus more than a matter of self-actualization. It is a matter of identification with God. This same issue is dealt with in I Peter: "Once you were no people but now you are God's people" (I Pet. 2:10).

To have a mark from God on one's forehead is not a new idea. In the very first book of the Bible, God places a mark on Cain after he had killed his brother Abel (Gen. 4:15). What is often overlooked is the fact that the mark on Cain was a preserving mark. John Steinbeck, in a novel of early California life, *East of Eden*, makes the Cain-Abel story the center of the plot. He writes: "Cain bore the mark not to destroy him but to save him. And there's a curse called down on any man who shall kill him. It was a preserving mark."[16]

We have noted earlier how Paul struggled with the people in Corinth over their tendency to follow particular leaders. It was as if they had on their foreheads the name *Apollos* or *Cephas* or *Paul* or even *Christ* (I Cor. 1:12). In a similar way in the counseling world, some counselors are so identified with a particular school of thought or a particular person that it is as if they had written on their foreheads *Frankl* or *Jung* or *Sullivan* or *Satir*. The real concern is not what particular person provides the leadership, but the degree to which one's spiritual growth is moving toward an alignment with God.

For God's name to be on a person's forehead suggests a claiming of God as being central in a person's life. And claiming God means power. Those who claim God shall reign (22:5) in an atmostphere where "there shall no more be anything accursed" (22:3). As the "Lamb" mediated the "light" as "lamp," so the "lampstands" (of each of the seven churches) will do what "clear glass" (not "a glass darkly") does without hindrance; namely, radiate, perhaps like spectral colors through a prism, the life-generating and life-sustaining "light." Twelve kinds of fruit (i.e., unending productivity) are nourished by the tree of life on either side of the river flowing through the city. God is seen dwelling with men and women, described in words that are almost a direct quotation from Ezekiel 37:27: "He will dwell with them, and they shall be his people, and God himself will be with them" (21:3). The holy city will have no need for the light of either the sun or the moon, "for the glory of God is its light" (21:23).[17]

Yet even in this picture of idyllic harmony, there is a realistic factor. There is no need for gates to keep things out (no repression of the dark side), but at the same time fulfillment includes a realistic recognition of right and wrong, of clean and unclean (21:25, 27).

Throughout this book we have recognized the tension between things as they are and things as they might be. The struggle between right and wrong is a never-ending one, and any useful psychological perspective needs to keep this in mind. Along with angel choruses, there are always Herods present. Thornton Wilder, in memorable lines in *The Skin of Our Teeth,* writes of this tension: "Oh, I've never forgotten for long at a time that living is struggle. I know that every good and excellent thing in the world stands moment by moment on the razor-edge of danger and must be fought for—whether it's a field, or a home, or a country."[18]

To claim God's name for oneself is not to eliminate problems. Throughout this book we have asserted that thorns are not taken away, that destructive powers remain potentially present. But when the good and the bad have been integrated, when the past and the future have been accepted, when the claim of God on one's life has been recognized, there is a release of power. Novelist Frederick Buechner concludes his novel *Lion Country* with a memorable affirmation of how in the death of his sister Miriam the best and the worst are mingled together.

> You cannot escape the past or the future either, and at my best and bravest I do not even want to escape them. . . . When Miriam's bones were breaking, for instance, if I could have pushed a button that would have stopped not her pain but the pain of her pain in me, I would not have pushed the button because, to put it quite simply, my pain was because I loved her, and to have wished my pain away would have been somehow to wish my love away as well. And at my best and bravest I do not want to escape the future either, even though I know that it contains what will someday be my own great and final pain. Because a distaste for dying is a twin to a taste for living, and again I don't think you can tamper with one without somehow doing mischief to the other.[19]

Perhaps the final surprise in the gospel is how all of life is related!

NOTES

1. Waiting / MATTHEW 1:18-25
A Gospel Lesson for the Fourth Sunday in Advent

1. Cf. John 1:13: ". . . born not of blood nor of the will of the flesh nor of the will of man, but of God." See also below, n. 10.
2. Cf. Fritz Kunkel: "Jesus is neither Joseph's son nor David's nor Abraham's; a new *'skandalon'*! From the ancient point of view, Jesus, not being the bodily offspring of Joseph, could not inherit the blessing and therefore could not be the potential messiah. The physical inheritance which we connect with the nobility of blood is missing." *Creation Continues: A Psychological Interpretation of the Gospel of Matthew* (Waco, Tex.: Word, [1946] 1973), 35. For special reference to the setting of the genealogies of Jesus, see Marshall D. Johnson, *The Purpose of Biblical Genealogies* (London: Cambridge University Press, 1969) and Herman C. Waetjen, *The Origin and Destiny of Humanness: An Interpretation of the Gospel According to Matthew* (Corte Madera, Calif.: Omega Books, 1976).
3. Cf. Fritz Kunkel: "Matthew's initial words 'Book of Genesis' repeat the title of the first book of the Old Testament. We are to witness a second Genesis, a re-beginning, a re-birth." *Creation Continues*, 33.
4. Unlike all the others in the genealogy, Jesus has no descendants. The story in both Matthew and Luke seems to contradict itself by first citing Joseph for the line of descent, then denying that Joseph was the biological father. Like all the others in the biblical genealogy, Jesus' "parents" and Jesus' "children" are those who "do the will of God / my Father" (Matt. 12:46-50, Mark 3:31-35, Luke 8:19-21, and the Gospel of Thomas 99).
5. Luke's parallel genealogy does not mention any of them (Luke 3:23-38). Regarding these four women, Marjorie Casebier McCoy notes that "the one thing that might tie them to

Mary is that each was involved in an unusual union that might have brought scorn from an outsider but which God used to carry forward the messianic line." *Mary, the Mother of Jesus* (Nashville: Graded Press, 1980), 34, student book.

6. Cf. Kunkel: "In the New Testament it [the Greek word *skandalon* = 'offence, hindrance, stumbling block'] always indicates a situation of great dynamic potentiality, a crossroads in history, the possibility of failure and deviation as well as of victory and spiritual growth." *Creation Continues,* 34. See Gustav Stählin, *"skandalon," Theological Dictionary of the New Testament,* ed. Gerhard Friedrich, trans. Geoffrey W. Bromiley (Grand Rapids: Wm. B. Eerdmans Publishing Co., 1971), 7:339-58, especially 346-52.

7. *Mary, the Mother of Jesus,* 14. See also Raymond Edward Brown, *The Birth of the Messiah* (Garden City, N.Y.: Doubleday, 1977).

8. Mary Ellen Chase, *Windswept* (New York: Macmillan, 1941), 261.

9. On waiting as "accept or receive," see Walter Grundmann, *"ek- or pros-dechesthai," Theological Dictionary of the New Testament* 2 (1964): 56-58; waiting as "expect or stand still," see Friedrich Hauck, *"perimenein,"* ibid., 4 (1967): 578-79; on "the tension of waiting as fear or hope," see Christian Mauer, *"prosdokasthai,"* ibid., 6 (1968): 725-27.

10. Geza Vermes, *Jesus the Jew: A Historian's Reading of the Gospels* (New York: Macmillan, 1973), 213-22. Note especially Jesus, son of Joseph (215-18), Jesus, son of a Virgin (218-20), and "marriage prior to puberty" (219-20).

11. Alternative translations further highlight the "sexist" behavior of this "righteous" or "pious" male: "he was minded to put her away privily" (King James); "he decided to break off the engagement privately" (Edgar J. Goodspeed, The Complete Bible: An American Translation, The University of Chicago Press. Copyright 1939 by the University of Chicago); "he decided to divorce her secretly" (Beck).

12. The cultures of the East tend to stress "shame," a community concept, while the cultures of the West tend to stress "guilt," an individual concept. See Bruce J. Malina, *The New Testament World: Insights from Cultural Anthropology* (Atlanta: John Knox Press, 1981), chap. 2, "Honor and Shame: Pivotal Values of the First-century Mediterranean World," 25-50. See also Robert C. Leslie, "Counseling Across Cultures," United Ministries in Higher Education Monograph Series Number 5, June 1979. Available from Educational Ministries, American Baptist Church, Valley Forge, Penn. 19481.

13. Matthew's account of the birth of Jesus is full of dreams and angels. See Joseph in 1:20-23 (marry Mary); 2:13 (flee to Egypt); 2:19 (return to Israel); 2:22 (go to Galilee). See also wise men in 2:12 (depart another way). On dreams in the Bible, see John A. Sanford, *Dreams: God's Forgotten Language* (Philadelphia: J. B. Lippincott Co., 1968), chap. 6, and Morton T. Kelsey, *Dreams: A Way to Listen to God* (New York: Paulist Press, 1978). See also Albert Oepke, *"onar,"* *Theological Dictionary of the New Testament* 5 (1967): 220-38; and Horst Balz, *"hypnos,"* ibid., 8 (1972): 545-56.

14. *Mary, the Mother of Jesus*, 22.

15. In 2:12, the wise men are also warned in a dream. For an illustration of dream interpretation, see pp. 125-26.

16. *Windswept*, 103-4.

17. *Creation Continues*, 36.

18. Viktor E. Frankl, Religion in Higher Education *Newsletter*, 20 October 1960, 5-6. Used by permission. For another account of this experience, see Frankl, "The Significance of Meaning for Health," in *Religion and Medicine: Essays on Meaning, Values and Health*, ed. David Belgum (Ames: Iowa State University Press, 1967), 184-85.

19. See 2:5, 15, 17, 23; 4:14; 8:17; 12:17; 13:35; 21:4; 26:56; 27:9.

20. Currently this people is characterized by "their sin" (missing the mark), as was the Exodus generation under Moses which died in their sins and did not enter the promised land. But under Joshua/Jesus a new people is led forth, a people of Jews and all nations, i.e., those who, like Abraham (as Israel's greatest "Gentile" convert!), were made righteous by faith.

21. Matthew quotes Isaiah 7:14 here.

22. Cf. Psalm 23: "Even though I walk through the valley of the shadow of death, I fear no evil; for thou art with me."

23. *Windswept*, 74-77.

24. For a realistic account of the contemporary struggle between the forces of good and evil, see Ernesto Cardénal, *The Gospel in Solentiname*, trans. Donald D. Walsh (Maryknoll, N.Y.: Orbis Books, [1976] 1982), 4 vols.

25. Viktor E. Frankl, *Man's Search for Meaning: An Introduction to Logotherapy* (New York: Pocket Books, 1963), 181-83. The first edition of this book published in English had the title *From Death-Camp to Existentialism* (1959).

26. Viktor E. Frankl, "The Will to Meaning," *Journal of Pastoral Care* 12 (Summer 1958), 87.

27. *Creation Continues*, 28.

28. For other symbols of Jesus used by Matthew, see 2:2, "king of the Jews"; 2:15, "out of Egypt have I called my son"; 2:23, "He shall be called a Nazarene"; 3:17, "This is my beloved son."
29. Arthur Miller, *After the Fall* (New York: Bantam World Drama, [1964] 1967), 5.
30. Ibid., 30-31. See also p. 118 above.
31. M. Scott Peck, *The Road Less Traveled: A New Psychology of Love, Traditional Values and Spiritual Growth* (New York: Simon & Schuster Touchstone, 1978), 302.
32. Ibid., 304.

2. Glorifying / LUKE 2:1-20
A Gospel Lesson for Christmas Day

1. Cf. Fritz Kunkel: "The contradictions between Luke's sweet harmonies and Matthew's shrill discord force us into a new meditation." *Creation Continues*, 38-39. Note also Marjorie Casebier McCoy's comment on a distinctive feature in Luke: "The Gospel of Luke parallels the accounts of John the Baptist and Jesus. Each time something marvelous is told about John, a more wondrous thing is told about Jesus; while John was conceived when his parents were very old, Jesus was conceived with no human father at all." *Mary, the Mother of Jesus*, 16.
2. Bethlehem, "the least among the cities of Judah" (Micah 5:2), yet rich with historical and cultural associations. See Gus W. Van Beek, "Bethlehem," *The Interpreter's Dictionary of the Bible* (Nashville: Abingdon Press), 1 (1962): 394-95.
3. Flavius Josephus, *The Jewish War*, Book 2, paragraph 60 on Athrongaeus the shepherd usurping the throne with the help of an armed band of shepherds.
4. Ann Belford Ulanov, *The Feminine in Jungian Psychology and in Christian Theology* (Evanston, Ill.: Northwestern University Press, 1971), 109.
5. Ann Conrad Lammers, "A Woman on the Docks," *Journal of Pastoral Care* 36 (December 1982): 221-22.
6. *Mary, the Mother of Jesus*, 28.
7. Ibid. McCoy goes on to note that "some of the paintings showing Isis with her baby god-king Horus enthroned on her knee have been mistaken for representations of Mary holding the baby Jesus."
8. For other references to the "Most High" see Luke 6:35, 8:28, 19:38; Acts 7:48, 16:17. See Georg Bertram, "hypsistos," *Theological Dictionary of the New Testament* 8 (1972): 614-20. Luke and Acts are assumed to have been written by the same author. See the salutation to Theophilus at the beginning of each of these books.

9. Sören Kierkegaard, *Either/Or* (Princeton, N.J.: Princeton University Press, [1843] 1944).

10. Both Matthew (22:37-38) and Mark (12:29-30) cite this as the "first" commandment.

11. M. Scott Peck, *The Road Less Traveled*, 197.

12. Ibid., 210.

13. On pleasing God *(eudokein)*, see Luke 3:22; 10:21; 12:32. See also *areskein*, I Thess. 4:1; I Cor. 7:32. See Gottlob Schrenk, *"eudokein," Theological Dictionary of the New Testament* 2 (1964): 738-51, especially 747-48 on Luke 2; Werner Foerster, *"areskein,"* ibid., 1 (1964): 455-57.

14. Ann Belford Ulanov, *Receiving Woman: Studies in the Psychology and Theology of the Feminine* (Philadelphia: The Westminster Press, 1981), 74.

15. L. Paul Trudinger, "The Bethlehem Inn Keeper: Heartless or Sensitive?" *Journal of Pastoral Care* 28 (December 1974): 219.

16. "Neurosis is always a substitute for legitimate suffering." See chap. 13, n. 15.

17. Roy W. Fairchild, "Pastor, Meet Dr. Jung," *Pacific Theological Review* 7 (Winter 1975): 5.

18. C. G. Jung, *Modern Man in Search of a Soul* (New York: Harcourt, Brace, 1934), 229.

19. On "fear" in Luke-Acts, see Luke 1:12, 1:65, 5:26, 7:16, 8:37, 21:26; Acts 2:43, 5:5, 5:11, 9:31, 19:17. On "Epiphany of God's Kingdom and Fears," see Horst Balz, *"phobos," Theological Dictionary of the New Testament* 9 (1974): 209-12; see also "faith and fear," 213-14. See chap. 8, n. 10 on "fear and trembling." See also chap. 5, n. 19.

20. On "joy" in Luke-Acts, see Luke 1:14, 8:13, 10:17, 15:7, 15:10, 24:41, 24:52; Acts 8:8, 12:14, 13:52, 15:3. On "joy (as) the state initiated by epiphany," see Hans G. Conzelmann, *"chara," Theological Dictionary of the New Testament* 9 (1974): 367-68.

21. Arthur Miller, *After the Fall*, 5.

22. Ibid.

23. *The Road Less Traveled*, 303.

24. Ibid.

25. The word *Emmanuel* is found only in Matthew 1:23. On the origin, history, and symbolism of the "name," see H. L. Ginsberg, "Immanuel," *Encyclopaedia Judaica* (New York: Macmillan), 8 (1971): 1293-95.

26. John Steinbeck, *East of Eden* (New York: Bantam Books, [1952] 1970), 150, 151.

27. Ibid., 670.

3. Refusing / MARK 5:1-20
A Gospel Lesson Appropriate for Epiphany

1. See 1:23-28; 1:32, 34; 3:11; 3:13-15; 3:20-23; 5:1-20 (this passage); 6:7, 13; 7:25-26, 29; 9:17-18, 25; 9:38; 16:17.
2. Cf. the novel made into a movie, Corbett H. Thigpen and Hervey M. Cleckley, *The Three Faces of Eve* (New York: McGraw-Hill, 1957).
3. Anne Frank, "The Diary of a Young Girl," *The Works of Anne Frank* (Garden City, N.Y.: Doubleday, 1959), 239.
4. John Sutherland Bonnell, "The Demoniac of Gerasa," *Pastoral Psychology* 7 (September 1956): 26. See also Colleen A. Ward and Michael H. Beaubrun, "The Psychodynamics of Demon Possession," *Journal for the Scientific Study of Religion* 19 (June 1980): 201-7.
5. Harry Stack Sullivan, *The Interpersonal Theory of Psychiatry* (New York: W. W. Norton & Co., 1953), 161-64.
6. Carroll Wise in a review of Harry Stack Sullivan, *The Psychiatric Interview,* in *Pastoral Psychology* 11 (November 1960): 34-35.
7. Theodore Isaac Rubin, *Jordi* and *Lisa and David* (New York: Ballantine Books, [1961] 1962), 75-130.
8. See also words spoken by other unclean spirits: "I know you are the Holy One of God" (1:24); "You are the Son of God" (3:11). On "the demons' recognition of the Messiah" in Mark 1:23-25; 1:34; 3:11-12; 5:6; and 9:20, see William Wrede, *The Messianic Secret,* trans. J. C. G. Greig (Greenwood, S.C.: Attic, 1971; from the original German, 1901), 24-34.
9. See the words of the familiar hymn by John Greenleaf Whittier:
   > Dear Lord and Father of mankind,
   > Forgive our foolish ways;
   > Reclothe us in our rightful mind,
   > In purer lives thy service find,
   > In deeper reverence, praise.
10. Form criticism discloses that Mark 5 is one of nine "novellen" or "tales" in Mark (1:40-45—leper; 4:35-41—storm; 5:1-20— this passage; 5:21-43—resurrection, but including the hemorrhaging woman; 6:35-44—feeding five thousand; 6:45-52—walking on water; 7:32-37—deaf-mute; 8:22-26—blind; 9:14-29—epileptic boy). All have three common features: (1) interest in descriptive details; (2) emphasis is not on a saying of Jesus, but on an act of power; (3) naiveté of tone. The act of power itself is never explained, even when its method is described; but always strongly emphasized is the effect on those who witnessed or heard of the action. See Martin

Dibelius, *From Tradition to Gospel* (New York: Scribner's, 1965; German original, 1919), chap. 4, "Tales," 70-103. For a different classification, see Werner H. Kelber, *The Oral and the Written Gospel* (Philadelphia: Fortress Press, 1983), chap. 2, distinguishing among "heroic" stories (46-52, i.e., healings), "polarization" stories (52-55, i.e., exorcisms, as in Mark 5), "didactic" stories (55-57; see "pronouncement" stories, chap. 12, n. 1) and "parabolic" stories (57-64).

11. Leslie Weatherhead suggests that when Jesus asked, "What is your name?" he was doing the equivalent of a psychotherapist's inquiry into a mental patient's past, leading eventually to a catharsis of a repressed, traumatic event. *Psychology, Religion, and Healing* (Nashville: Abingdon Press, 1951), 55.

12. Rollo May, *Love and Will* (New York: W. W. Norton & Co., 1969), 123.

13. Fritz Kunkel, *Creation Continues*, 126.

14. Norman Perrin sees Mark 5:1-20 as a part of the "Second Major Section [of Mark]: Jesus as Son of God, and as rejected by his own people" (3:13–6:6a). Perrin's student, Werner H. Kelber *(The Kingdom in Mark,* Philadelphia: Fortress Press, 1974, chap. 3) sees our story as part of the expansion and unity of the kingdom. See also Kelber, *The Oral and the Written Gospel* (Philadelphia: Fortress Press, 1983), 106 on how Mark, in 3–6, creates a comprehensive narrative out of many oral strands.

15. Bruno Bettelheim, *Love Is Not Enough: The Treatment of Emotionally Disturbed Children* (Glencoe, Ill.: Free Press, 1950).

16. In the Asian culture, however, there is a great reluctance to say no. Many Westerners are astonished to discover to what lengths business people in Asia, for example, will go to avoid saying no in specific terms, even though the intent is to give a negative answer.

17. James Dittes, *When the People Say No* (New York: Harper & Row, 1979).

18. Cf. 1:34 (to demons); 5:37 (to some disciples).

19. These words are in the stage directions, Arthur Miller, *After the Fall,* 163.

4. Confronting / JOHN 4:1-42
A Gospel Lesson for the Second Sunday in Lent

1. For a similar situation, see p. 111.

2. Cf. Luke 9:51-56: "a village of the Samaritans would not receive him." On the escalating estrangement, then hostility, and finally schism, between Judean and Samaritan Jews, see Theodor H. Gaster, "Samaritans," *The Interpreter's Dictionary of the Bible* 4 (1962): 190-97, and James D. Purvis' update in *The*

Interpreter's Dictionary of the Bible, Supplementary Volume (Nashville: Abingdon Press, 1976): 776-77. See also Joachim Jeremias, "Samareia," *Theological Dictionary of the New Testament* 7 (1971): 88-94.

3. See chap. 2, n. 16.

4. John's symbolism in his prologue is more abstract or mythological than is the symbolism of Matthew (wise men) or Luke (shepherds) as described in chaps. 1 and 2.

5. Irene M. Josselyn, "Psychological Aspects of Adolescence," *American Journal of Orthopsychiatry* 26 (July 1956): 481.

6. The well, as a symbol, suggests the dimension of depth. Water, for the Samaritan woman, was symbolic of her spiritual thirst just as food, for the disciples, was symbolic of their spiritual hunger (4:31-34). There is also a special cultural significance to a well in a land surrounded by desert. Moreover, this well was a very special well. It was Jacob's well, a special place to make contact with religious history. To go to Jacob's well was like making a pilgrimage to the Lincoln Memorial in Washington, D.C., as Martin Luther King, Jr., did in the Freedom March on August 28, 1963.

7. Virginia Satir, *Peoplemaking: So You Want to Be a Better Parent* (Palo Alto: Science and Behavior Books, 1972).

8. The story ends with a focus not just on a Savior of Jews or of Samaritans but on "the Savior of the world" (4:42). See also 3:16, "For God so loved the world . . ."

9. See chap. 3.

10. Paul Tournier, *The Meaning of Persons* (New York: Harper & Brothers, 1957), 198-99.

11. Reuel L. Howe, *Herein Is Love* (Philadelphia: Judson Press, 1961), 40, citing the dialogue between Brick and Big Daddy at the end of Act Two, Tennessee Williams, *Cat On a Hot Tin Roof* (New York: Signet Books, [1955] 1958). Note especially "Person-to-Person," vii-x.

12. Cf. Robert C. Leslie, *Jesus as Counselor* (Nashville: Abingdon Press, [1965]; Abingdon Press Festival Book, 1982), 49.

13. Both the Samaritan woman and the disciples experience the existential vacuum. The vacuum is due to doing one's own will and accomplishing one's own work. To have living water and food is to do the will of God. See p. 143, n. 1 on Fiorenza.

14. See John 1:1, "In the beginning was the word [*logos*]." For the full connotation of the Greek *logos* concept, see the article *"legein/logos,"* in *Theological Dictionary of the New Testament* 4 (1967): 69-143, especially 127-36 on John's Gospel; or Raymond E. Brown, *The Gospel According to John, The Anchor Bible* (Garden City, N.Y.: Doubleday, 1966), 29: cxxii-cxxv on *logos* and Old Testament motifs.

15. Viktor E. Frankl specifies three dimensions for finding meaning, each one more inclusive than the previous one: creative values (creating something), experiential values (experiencing something or someone), and attitudinal values (taking an attitudinal stand). See *The Doctor and the Soul: From Psychotherapy to Logotherapy* (New York: Vintage Books, [1955] 1973), 43-44.

16. From an interview recorded in a lecture-classroom demonstration in Vienna, Spring 1961. Quoted in *Jesus as Counselor,* 62-63.

5. Healing / MATTHEW 9:1-8
A Gospel Lesson Appropriate for Lent

1. In the Gospel parallels the same story appears in Mark 2:1-12, Luke 5:17-20, and John 5:1-9. Matthew's version, which we are using, is shorter than the others. It is firmly embedded in a series of three events: it is followed by the story of Jesus' association with sinners (tax-collectors), and by the controversy about fasting, climaxing in the saying about old and new wineskins.

2. See Morton T. Kelsey, *Healing and Christianity: In Ancient Thought and Modern Times* (New York: Harper & Row, 1976).

3. On "Forgiveness," see Warren A. Quanbeck, *The Interpreter's Dictionary of the Bible* 2 (1962): 314-19.

4. Cited by Flanders Dunbar, *Mind and Body: Psychosomatic Medicine* (New York: Random House, 1947), 31.

5. Henry Denker, *A Far Country: A New Play* (New York: Random House, 1961).

6. Arthur Miller, *The Price* (New York: Bantam World Drama, [1968] 1969), 16.

7. Ibid., 107.

8. For other faith references in Matthew, see 9:22, 29; 15:28; 17:20 (like mustard seed); 21:21 (never doubting); 23:23 (justice, mercy, faith as "the weightier matters of the law"). See also the use of the verb *to believe.* On "Faith, Faithfulness in the New Testament," see John Reumann's article in *The Interpreter's Dictionary of the Bible,* Supplementary Volume (1976): 332-35, especially 333 on Matthew.

9. In Jesus' own city, Capernaum (4:13, 8:5, 11:23, 17:24; cf. his own country 13:57), "they" bring him someone crippled (weakened or paralyzed, literally "dissolved"—*para-luo;* 4:24, 8:6, and here). On paralysis as "one of the diseases of the New Testament," see R. K. Harrison, *The Interpreter's Dictionary of the Bible* 1 (1962), 851-52. See below, n. 12. There is "faith" in

Israel (see 8:10, "not even in Israel have I found such faith"). On the five different aspects of faith which "general Christian usage" has in common with Old Testament and Jewish traditions, see Rudolf Bultmann, *"pisteuein," Theological Dictionary of the New Testament* 6 (1968): 205-8 (and 215-17).

10. Jerome Frank, *Persuasion and Healing* (Baltimore: Johns Hopkins University Press, [1961] 1973), chap. 3. On "the cloud of witnesses," i.e., the supportive social, communal setting for therapy to occur, see anthropologist Ailon Shiloh's "paradigm [for interpreting] the dynamics of faith healing," in his book *Faith Healing: The Religious Experience as a Therapeutic Process* (Springfield, Ill.: Thomas, 1981), 51-68.

11. The text with its emphasis on healing and on resistance is part of a larger unit (4:18–13:58) which has the same two foci: the healing ministry of Jesus and the growing opposition. The whole larger unit ends on the opposition note: due to the unbelief, there is no more healing in the therapist's own home and country (13:58). See Jack Dean Kingsbury, *Matthew*. Proclamation Commentaries, ed. Gerhard Krodel (Philadelphia: Fortress Press, 1977), 21-29. On "the cultural factors that account for [both the revival or decline of interest in the supernatural in therapy]," see Theodore Ziolkowski, *Disenchanted Images: A Literary Iconology* (Princeton, N.J.: Princeton University Press, 1977), 227-57; see also Klaus Seybold and Ulrich B. Mueller, *Sickness and Healing*. Biblical Encounter Series (Nashville: Abingdon Press, 1981), 9-13.

12. On disease as punishment for sin, see Harrison's essay cited above, n. 9.

13. Lawrence LeShan, *You Can Fight For Your Life: Emotional Factors in the Causation of Cancer* (New York: Jove/Harcourt Brace Jovanovich, 1978), 69.

14. Newman S. Cryer, Jr., and John Monroe Vayhinger, *Casebook in Pastoral Counseling* (Nashville: Abingdon Press, 1962), 44–47.

15. John C. Whitehorn in foreword to Jerome Frank, *Persuasion and Healing*, 1961 ed., vii.

16. Leslie Weatherhead, *It Happened in Palestine* (New York: Abingdon Press, 1936) writes: "The same Greek word was often used by Saint Paul as a term of endearment. He used it of Timothy. See II Tim. 1:2. Cf. also Philemon 10. Note the same word in III John 4," 93. See also J. T. Holland, who writes of Jesus: "By addressing people by their first names or other endearing terms, he indicated the affection and sense of dignity by which he regarded them." "Jesus, a Model for Ministry,"*Journal of Pastoral Care* 36 (December 1982): 262.

17. Viktor E. Frankl, *Trotzdem Ja zum Leben sagen* (Wien: Franz Deuticke, 1947).

18. Norman Cousins, *Anatomy of an Illness As Perceived by the Patient: Reflections on Healing and Regeneration* (New York: W. W. Norton & Co., 1979).

19. Cf. the Gerasenes demoniac in chap. 3.

20. This combination of two "forms," miracle and controversy, is unusual. It stresses how difficult change is. Cf. Walter Wink, who notes the scribe in each of us, i.e., that feature "endemic to all religions wherever blame or moral standards are established." *The Bible in Human Transformation: A New Paradigm for Biblical Study* (Philadelphia: Fortress Press, 1973), 55, n. 43. Wink also invites readers to identify how they, too, are paralyzed, 56ff. On "scribes," see Matthew Black, *The Interpreter's Dictionary of the Bible* 4 (1962): 246-48.

21. Blasphemy: first mentioned here; also 26:65 and 27:39; and blasphemy of the Spirit in 12:31. In 15:19, "slander" is one of the things which comes out of the heart. The high priest's charge of blasphemy in 26:65 is in response to Jesus' quoting of Dan. 7:13 (seeing the Son of man sitting . . . and coming . . .). See Simon J. DeVries, "Blasphemy," *The Interpreter's Dictionary of the Bible* 1 (1962): 445.

    Such "evil thoughts" are discerned by Jesus twice in Matthew: here and in 12:25. On "what is easier," see 19:24 ("easier for a camel to go through the eye of a needle").

22. There are twenty-one references to fear in Matthew. "Fear" may sometimes appear as a constitutive element of faith; on this see chap. 2, n. 19.

23. Fritz Kunkel, *Creation Continues*, 128.

24. Ibid., 129.

6. Denying / MARK 14:66-72
A Gospel Lesson for the Sixth Sunday in Lent

1. See also 6:51; 7:36.

2. Cf. the women who looked on "from afar" (15:40). See also 5:6; 8:3; 11:13. "At a distance" suggests a symbolic act which implies avoiding, repressing, denouncing. See Psalm 38:11, ". . . my kinsmen" or "even the dearest of [my friends]" (Jerusalem Bible) "stand afar off," i.e., "keep their distance." "The severity of his suffering is augmented by the conduct toward him of his intimate and trusted friends. . . . Those from whom he might normally expect sympathy stand aloof. He feels isolated and alone. . . . Turning a deaf ear [to his friends'] false and baseless indictments, he looks expectantly to

his God in certainty of His answering help." Elmer A. Leslie, *The Psalms* (Nashville: Abingdon Press, 1949), 374.

3. Fritz Kunkel sees the key to Matthew's Gospel, too, in Peter: "While reading the first Gospel, we should constantly ask . . . 'What happens to Peter?' rather than, 'What happens to Jesus?' " *Creation Continues,* 23. See also *Peter in the New Testament,* ed. Raymond E. Brown, Karl P. Donfried, John Reumann (Minneapolis: Augsburg Publishing House, 1973), 57-73 on Peter in Mark; 75-107 on Peter in Matthew.

4. On "Mark as Textuality," see Werner H. Kelber, *The Oral and the Written Gospel,* 91-106, with the "text" becoming a "written parable," 117-29, and an "agent of alienation and liberation," 129-31.

5. Eric Berne, *Games People Play* (New York: Grove Press, 1964). Even more help than this popular account of T. A. is Muriel James and Dorothy Jongeward's best seller, *Born to Win: Transactional Analysis with Gestalt Experiments* (Reading, Mass.: Addison-Wesley, 1971).

6. Viktor E. Frankl, *The Doctor and the Soul,* 90.

7. See Robert C. Leslie, "Mobilizing the Defiant Power of the Human Spirit," chap. 2 in *Jesus as Counselor.*

8. Ken Kesey, *One Flew Over the Cuckoo's Nest* (New York: Viking Compass, [1962] 1964), 24.

9. Ibid., 136.

10. For a poetic representation of this moment, see Clive Sansom, "Peter," in *The Witnesses and Other Poems* (London: Methuen, 1956), 23-25.

11. See chap. 5, n. 16.

12. For other "bystanders" see 14:47 (drawing a sword) and 15:35 (interpreting Jesus' death cry).

13. Matthew adds that Peter's second denial was made "with an oath" when a second maid joined in with her accusation. On the triad in the denial as part of the "folkloristic triads," and the use of the historical present (as, for example in 14:67, which reads in literal translation: "the maid looked at Peter and *says*") as means of magnifying "the gospel's dramatic intensity," see *The Oral and the Written Gospel,* 65-66.

14. On "this man," see also 2:7; 4:41; 6:3; 15:39, with a connotation of contempt or dissociation.

15. Excerpts from "The Day Dag Hammarskjöld Rode in My Jeep," by Jhan Robbins, *Reader's Digest,* May 1962.

16. For the Last Supper scene, Luke adds: "This do in remembrance of me" (Luke 22:19). In Luke's account of the denial story, he adds: "The Lord turned and looked at Peter" (Luke 22:61). We would judge the look to be one of love and

not one of condemnation. See the painting *Peter's Denial*, by Count von Ferdinand Harrach, painted in 1879 and hanging in the art museum in Breslau, Germany. For a copy of the picture and a discussion, see Cynthia Pearl Maus, *Christ and the Fine Arts* (New York: Harper & Brothers, 1938), 329-33. On Peter in Luke's Gospel, see *Peter in the New Testament*, 109-28.

17. On tears, see also 5:38-39; 16:10. Peter "began to weep," or "broke down and wept." On emotional varieties and degrees and intensity of weeping, as reflected in seven different Greek terms employed in the New Testament, see Heinrich Rengstorf, *"klaio," Theological Dictionary of the New Testament* 3 (1965): 722-26, especially 724-25. The patristic church even developed a "sacrament of tears"!

18. See Domini Clare Collins, "Pastoral Counselors and the Crying Woman: A Study of Difference in Responses Between Male and Female Pastoral Counselors" (Ph.D. diss., Graduate Theological Union, Berkeley, Calif., 1980).

19. The word is used in this sense only in this passage. The meaning of the original Greek phrase used in Mark 14:72 is in doubt. William F. Arndt and F. Wilbur Gingrich propose the following options: (1) Peter covers his head and weeps; (2) he began to weep; (3) he thought of it—or, when he reflected on it—and wept; (4) he responded by weeping. *A Greek-English Lexicon of the New Testament and Other Early Christian Literature* (Chicago: University of Chicago Press, 2 ed., 1979), 290.

20. Stanley W. Standal and Raymond J. Corsini, eds., *Critical Incidents in Psychotherapy* (Englewood Cliffs, N.J.: Prentice-Hall, 1959), 1.

21. Ibid., 2-3.

22. Ibid., 3.

7. Washing / JOHN 13:1-15
A Gospel Lesson for Maundy Thursday

1. See chap. 4 above.

2. The story in John brings out the immediate and the ultimate meaning by narrating and interpreting the event and its accompanying teaching in the following order. The first verse calls attention to the larger context of this event, seeing it as the introduction to the second half of John's Gospel (chaps. 13–21). The following four verses, which are actually one sentence, introduce the setting of the act (verses 4-5) which later (verse 15) gets recognized as an "example." Finally, in ten more verses, we are offered an interpretation of the meaning of this symbol—first by an actual dialogue with Peter (verses

6-10*a*) and a concluding reference to the traitor Judas (verses 10*b*-11), which links this interpretation with the opening "setting" of the story in verse 2 and with the return to Judas in verses 18-19—and by an implied dialogue with all disciples (verses 12-15).

3. For the foot-washing as one of Jesus' several "symbolic" or "parabolic" actions, see Joachim Jeremias, *The Parables of Jesus* (New York: Scribner's, 1963), 227-29.

4. See Mark 9:33-37, Matt. 18:1-5, and Luke 9:46-48; also Mark 10:42-45, Matt. 20:25-28, and Luke 22:24-30.

5. Harry Stack Sullivan took a strong stand against psychological determinism, believing that the opportunity for change and growth is always present. He wrote: "I am conspicuously taking exception to the all-too-prevalent idea that things are pretty well fixed in the Jesuitical first seven years. . . . The development of capacity for interpersonal relations is by no means a matter which is completed at some point." *Conceptions of Modern Psychiatry* (New York: W. W. Norton & Co., 1940), 99.

6. Cf. the blowing wind as spirit rebirth in John 3; well water as stilling the thirst for life in John 4; food as eternal satisfaction in John 6.

7. Like John the Baptist's ministry of water baptism (1:31), Jesus' ministry of cleansing was a way of revealing the true Paschal Lamb, the Lamb of God, and our share or participation in it.

8. See chap. 10, n. 6.

9. Leave-taking in John starts with 5:13 (withdraw/*ekneuein*); 6:15 (withdraw/*anachorein*); 7:3-9 (time is not yet for leaving/*metabainein*); 10:39 (escaping/*exerchesthai*); 11:54 (no longer appearing openly/*parrhesia*); 12:36 (hiding) and then the leave-taking/farewell speech in chaps. 13–17.

10. See Sandra Schneiders, "The Footwashing (John 13:1-20): An Experiment in Hermeneutics," *Catholic Biblical Quarterly* 43 (1981): 76-92.

11. Cf. 15:15, "No longer do I call you servants . . . but I have called you friends." The divine emptying itself and becoming a servant, thus transforming servants to friends, was also expressed in Paul's Epistle to the Philippians 2:5-8.

12. I John 1:1 echoes this reference to hearing, seeing, touching; and we would add tasting and smelling. See also above, n. 6.

13. Thornton Wilder, *The Eighth Day* (New York: Harper & Row, 1967), 16.

14. On "shadow" see chap. 13.

15. Mark 8:33, Matt. 16:23, but not Luke.

16. *The Eighth Day*, 338.

17. See I Tim. 5:10.
18. Brock Chisholm in *Psychiatry* 12 (1949): 435.
19. Quoted by Arnold F. Emch, *Psychiatry* 12 (1949): 435.
20. Cf. Harry Stack Sullivan: "The benefits of treatment come in large part from their learning to notice what they are doing, and this is greatly expedited by carefully validated verbal statements as to what seems to be going on." *Conceptions of Modern Psychiatry*, 223.

8. Preparing / MARK 16:1-8
A Gospel Lesson for Easter Sunday

1. It is widely accepted that Mark's Gospel ends with 16:8 and that verses 9-20 are a later addition. See C. E. B. Cranfield, in *The Interpreter's Dictionary of the Bible* 3 (1962): 275-76 on "The Problem of the Ending." On the significance of "the *written* gospel [concluding] with the narration of the abortive mission of the *oral* message," see Werner H. Kelber, *The Oral and the Written Gospel*, 104. Where Kelber sees no redeeming role for the woman (see p. 108), a different view is offered by Elisabeth Schüssler Fiorenza, *In Memory of Her: A Feminist Theological Reconstruction of Christian Origins* (New York: Crossroad, 1983), 316-23.
2. Fritz Kunkel, *Creation Continues*, 275.
3. Note Mark's use of this way of designating Jesus: first in the mouth of a demoniac (1:24), then in the mouth of the high priest's maid (14:67), and here in the mouth of the "young man" (16:6). Cf. 10:47 (Luke 18:37) when blind Bartimaeus is told by the crowd about the Nazareth man.
4. This anointing was anticipated by an anonymous woman in the home of Simon the leper (14:3-9, also Matt. 26:6-13) at Bethany (cf. John 12:1-8 in the house of Mary and Martha, with Mary as the one who does it). Still another setting is in Luke 7:36-50.
5. Arthur Miller, *After the Fall*, 6. Cf. Sigmund Freud: "It may be universally observed that man never willingly abandons a libido position." "Mourning and Melancholia," *Collected Papers of Sigmund Freud*, ed. Ernest Jones (London: The Hogarth Press, [1917] 1925), 4: 154.
6. Thornton Wilder, *The Eighth Day*, 14.
7. *Creation Continues*, 275.
8. The young man in 16:5 may be related to the young man in 14:51. See the article by John Knox, "A Note on Mark 14:51-52," *The Joy of Study*, ed. Sherman E. Johnson (New York: Macmillan, 1951), 27-30; also Harry T. Fleddermann,

"The Flight of the Naked Young Man (Mark 14:51-52)," *Catholic Biblical Quarterly* 41 (1979): 412-18.

9. See parallel passages in Luke 24:4 (two men in "dazzling apparel") and in Matt. 28:2, 3 ("an angel . . ." whose "appearance was like lightning, and his raiment white as snow"). Note also Mark's account of the transfiguration of Jesus in which "his garments became glistening, intensely white" (9:3).

10. For "fear and trembling" see also I Cor. 2:3; II Cor. 7:15; Eph. 6:5; Phil. 2:12. On fear as part of faith, see chap. 2, n. 19.

11. For the women to be "afraid" in the "shorter Mark" is not the same as "unbelief and hardness of heart" in the longer Mark (16:14). For Kelber, *The Oral and the Written Gospel,* 128-29, the commission given to the women arouses hopes "one last time . . . that [they] might repair the broken connection, transmit the message of life, and facilitate the disciples' rehabilitation. But inasmuch as the narrative kindles such hopes, it does everything to wreck them." Like the disciples, the women "flee." With the disciples' and the women's "demise the structure of expectancy is finally and irrevocably reversed, and the narrative [i.e., all of Mark] has found its proper, parabolic ending. . . . Far from inviting us to settle for familiar, classical perspectives [i.e., 'happy' endings], [the parable] shocks us out of them toward a new and unfamiliar logic."

12. The disciples had "asked" Jesus for answers in 4:10, 7:17, 9:11, and 9:28. Though here, at one time, they were "afraid to ask," they resume asking twice more, 10:10 and 13:3. In 12:34 "no one dared to ask him any question"; in John 21:12, the disciples don't even dare ask the seeming stranger, "Who are you?" even though "they knew it was the Lord."

13. M. Scott Peck, *The Road Less Traveled,* 211.

14. Ibid., 221.

15. Ibid., 222.

16. Cf. the women's remaining at a distance ("looking on from afar") with the disciples' running away ("forsook him, and fled"), 14:50. See chap. 6, n. 2.

17. Papias, a mid-second century bishop, refers to Mark as Peter's "interpreter"; Justin Martyr speaks of Mark's Gospel as Peter's "memoirs." See C. E. B. Cranfield, "Mark," *The Interpreter's Dictionary of the Bible* 3 (1962): 267-68. On the premise of "early Christian traditions (as willing but) progressive development and continuity" (e.g., between Peter and Mark), see Kelber, *The Oral and the Written Gospel,* 211-20: This model of scholarship and ecclesiastical policy "has hampered more than

helped our comprehension of the written gospel and its relation to tradition," (212).

18. Alan Paton, *Too Late the Phalarope* (New York: Scribner's, 1953), 1.

9. Rejoicing / I PETER 1:3-9
An Epistle Lesson for the Second Sunday after Easter

1. Cf. Paul: "We rejoice in our suffering, knowing that suffering produces endurance, and endurance produces character, and character produces hope" (Rom. 5:3-4).

2. Harry Stack Sullivan combines subjective identification with objective analysis in the term which he uses to describe the role of the therapist: "participant-observer." *The Psychiatric Interview* (New York: W. W. Norton & Co., 1945), 19-25.

3. The "dispersion" refers to "the widespread settlement of Jews outside Palestine" since the Exile. See J. Alvin Sanders, "Dispersion," *The Interpreter's Dictionary of the Bible* 1 (1962): 854-56. On the Christian church as the twelve tribes in exile, see Karl L. Schmidt, *"diaspora," Theological Dictionary of the New Testament* 2 (1964): 98-104, especially 102ff; also ibid., 5 (1967): 841-53, especially 851ff. On "Babylon," (I Pet. 5:13) as synonym for "dispersion," see John H. Elliott, *A Home for the Homeless* (Philadelphia: Fortress Press, 1981), 37-49.

4. Although the God of I Peter is very masculine ("God the Father," 1:2 and "God and Father," 1:3), the attributes of God are described as "mercy" (1:3) as well as "power" (1:5), female and male polarities in equal proportions.

5. "Apocalypse" means not just "the basic possibility of communication from God to man," but rather God's free and continuing communication with humankind "from the beginning of the [biblical] story" to its very consummation. See James Barr, "Revelation in History," *The Interpreter's Dictionary of the Bible*, Supplementary Volume (1976): 746-49. For more exegetical details, see Albrecht Oepke, *"apokalypsis," Theological Dictionary of the New Testament* 3 (1965): 563-92: "Revelation denotes, not the impartation of knowledge, but the actual unveiling of intrinsically hidden facts, or, theologically, the manifestation of transcendence within immanence" (591); "The disclosure which corresponds to the concealment[!] begins with the resurrection and exaltation of Christ, continues through the Messianic *kerygma* [or spiritual, pastoral counseling], and will culminate with the *parousia*" (584). On "parousia" see below, n. 12.

6. See pp. 69 and 75.
7. See also chap. 14.
8. See John Marsh in Karl Barth, *Deliverance to the Captives* (New York: Harper & Brothers, 1961), 8 (preface).
9. Ibid., 9.
10. Ibid., 7.
11. See also I Pet. 2:12; 3:13-16; 4:2, 12-19; 5:6-10.
12. The "parousia" refers to the future and ultimate disclosure of the "fullness" of Christ. "The *parousia* is the definitive manifestation of what has been effected already as an eschatological reality . . . [it] is not a historical event; nor does it merely give history its goal and meaning. It is rather the point where history is mastered by God's eternal rule. The significance of the New Testament *parousia* concept is that the tension between non-fulfillment and fulfillment, . . . between faith and sight, should be resolved, and that the decisive contribution towards this has already been made in Christ," Albrecht Oepke, "parousia," *Theological Dictionary of The New Testament* 5 (1967): 858-71, especially the "Theological Summary," 870. See ibid., 2 (1964): 943-53 on "The Day," and 9 (1974): 7-10 on "Epiphany" or "Appearance." When "the perfect" *(teleios)* comes (I Cor. 13:10), only then shall we "be like [God] for [only then] shall we see [God] as he is" (I John 3:2-3).
13. M. Scott Peck, *The Road Less Traveled,* 15, 16.
14. It was Gordon Allport who introduced Viktor Frankl to the reading public in America by writing an enthusiastic endorsement to Frankl's *Man's Search for Meaning.* See Allport's preface in that book.
15. Gordon W. Allport, "The Trend in Motivational Theory," in *The Self: Explorations in Personal Growth,* ed. Clark E. Moustakas (New York: Harper & Brothers, 1956), 40-41.
16. Ibid., 41.
17. Cf. Mark on "fear and trembling" in chap. 8.
18. *The Unheard Cry for Meaning* (New York: Simon & Schuster, 1978), 38.
19. Quoted by Roy W. Fairchild in a review of *Psychological Reflections,* ed. Jolande Jacobi (New York: Pantheon Books, 1951) in *Journal of Pastoral Care* 11 (Fall 1957): 174.
20. Harry Stack Sullivan, *The Fusion of Psychiatry and Social Science* (New York: W. W. Norton & Co., 1964), 331.
21. Virginia Satir, *Peoplemaking,* 8.
22. Kim Chi Ha, *The Gold-Crowned Jesus and Other Writings* (Maryknoll, N.Y.: Orbis Books, 1978), 40.

23. Arthur Miller, *The Crucible* (New York: Bantam World Drama, [1952] 1966).
24. *Webster's Third New International Dictionary* (Springfield, Mass.: G. & C. Merriam, 1981), 545.
25. *The Crucible*, 138.
26. See p. 69.
27. Peter writes here as one who *has* seen Christ, but note John 20:29, "Have you believed because you have seen me? Blessed are those who have not seen and yet believe," or II Cor. 5:7, "We walk by faith, not by sight."
28. Richard Francis Weymouth, *The New Testament in Modern Speech* (Boston: The Pilgrim Press, n. d.), 565, Pocket Ed.
29. William James, *The Varieties of Religious Experience* (London: Longmans, Green & Co., [1902] 1915), 248 ff.
30. Arthur Miller, *After the Fall*, 8.
31. Ibid., 6.
32. *Peoplemaking*, 26.

10. Enabling / ACTS 2:1-21
An Epistle Lesson for Pentecost

1. Elizabeth Barrett Browning, "Aurora Leigh," *Poetical Works of Elizabeth B. Browning* (New York: A. L. Burt, 1887), 123.
2. The extraordinary time, the festival of Pentecost, was the second of three Jewish festivals which brought pilgrims to Jerusalem. *Pentecost* (the Greek word for "fifty") was a harvest festival coming on the fiftieth day after the second day of the feast of Passover, and was associated with the giving of the Torah from Sinai, following the Exodus from Egypt. (The first harvest festival was Passover; the third was Tabernacles.) The outset of the story is thus marked by the commemoration of God's activity in the past, and the promise of future activity associated with the prophecy of Joel.
3. Traditionally Luke and Acts are the work of the same author. See Henry J. Cadbury, "Acts of the Apostles," *The Interpreter's Dictionary of the Bible* 1 (1962): 38.
4. Mary Ellen Chase, *Windswept*, 47.
5. The words are by Marcus D. Buell.
6. This is not the familiar "speaking in tongues" *(glossolalia)* criticized by Paul in I Cor. 13:1 and also chap. 14 since *there* the words were unintelligible, but *here* the words are quite specific foreign languages. See Elias Andrews, "Tongues, Gift of," *The Interpreter's Dictionary of the Bible* 4 (1962): 671-72; and Earle E. Ellis, ibid., Supplementary Volume (1976): 908-9.

7. *Windswept,* 440.
8. On the political, cultural contest between "East and West" (Asia and Europe), see Mark J. Dresden, "Persia," *The Interpreter's Dictionary of the Bible* 3 (1962): 744, and Robert M. Grant, "Roman Empire," ibid., 4 (1962): 103-4.
9. Harry Stack Sullivan, *The Fusion of Psychiatry and Social Science,* 330.
10. Elisabeth Kübler-Ross, *Living With Death and Dying* (New York: Macmillan, 1981), 20-21.
11. Peter speaks particularly to only one of many groups, the Judeans who are Jerusalemites. See Kenneth W. Clark, "Judea," *The Interpreter's Dictionary of the Bible* 2 (1962): 1011-12.

    Note, too, that with appropriate psychological insight, he does not ignore the mockers (2:13) but deals with them first (2:15).
12. Thornton Wilder, *The Eighth Day,* 197.
13. James B. Ashbrook, "The Name of the Game: Babel—Legion—Pentecost," *Journal of Pastoral Care* 36 (June 1982): 121-22.
14. *Windswept,* 54.
15. The word "boldness" *(parrhesia)* has a double connotation: "fearless," i.e., having come to terms with the ominous and the threatening, and "openness," vulnerable and hence capable of being changed. The word is used many times: as a noun in 2:29, 4:13, 4:29, 4:31, 28:31; as an adverb in 14:3, 18:26, 19:8, and 26:26; as a verb (only of Paul) in 9:27, 29, 13:41b. See Paul E. Davies, "Boldness," *The Interpreter's Dictionary of the Bible* 1 (1962): 453, and W. Ward Gasque, ibid., Supplementary Volume (1976): 118-19. See also Heinrich Schlier in *Theological Dictionary of the New Testament* 5 (1967): 882, on "boldness" in Acts as *"charisma."*
16. Joel 2:28-32. The promising element in Joel's prophecy is cited also in Romans 10:13. The destructive element in Joel's prophecy is echoed in several chapters of the Revelation to John: in the opening of the seven seals (chaps. 6 and 7) and in the sounding of the seven trumpets (chaps. 8 and 9).
17. James Muilenberg in *The Choice Is Always Ours,* ed. Dorothy Berkeley Phillips (New York: Richard R. Smith, 1951), 9.
18. Viktor E. Frankl, *The Doctor and the Soul,* 58.

11. Laughing / II CORINTHIANS 11:21b–12:10
An Epistle Lesson for the Seventh Sunday after Pentecost

1. For another place where Paul's humor comes through, see p. 114.

148

2. II Cor. 11:21*b*–12:10 is a part of the Apostle's "fool's speech"
(11:5–12:13), which in turn is part of the "letter of tears"
(chaps. 10–13), which in turn is now part of the "body middle"
of the whole "second" letter to the Corinthians (II Cor.
1:12–13:10). On the problem of the unity of II Corinthians as a
whole, see S. McLean Gilmore, "Corinthians, Second," *The
Interpreter's Dictionary of the Bible* 1 (1962): 694-95; Dieter
Georgi, ibid., Supplementary Volume (1976): 183-84. On the
history and motivation of combining Paul's "several letters"
into II Corinthians as a unity, see Charles K. Barrett, *A
Commentary on the Second Epistle to the Corinthians* (New York:
Harper & Row, 1973), 22-35.
3. On other comments about the "fools for Christ" approach to
life and growth, see the following texts: I Cor. 1:18-31
(followed by an autobiographical example in 2:1-5), 4:6-21; II
Cor. 4:7-18, 6:1-10; Gal. 6:17; Rom. 5:3-5; James 1:2-4, 1:12,
5:7-8. See also Hebrews and I Peter yet without humor; but in
the Revelation to John with at least occasional "irony." On
Paul's use and understanding of being "foolish," see Dieter
Georgi, "Folly," *The Interpreter's Dictionary of the Bible,*
Supplementary Volume (1976): 340-41. On the role of
"Humor," and "Irony and Satire" in the religious experience,
see W. F. Stinespring, ibid., 2 (1962): 660-62, and 726-28. See
also Hud J. Jonsson, *Humour and Irony in the New Testament*
(Reykjavík: Bókaútgáfa Menningarsjóds, 1965).
4. Thornton Wilder, *The Eighth Day*, 430.
5. Ibid.
6. Ibid.
7. Cf. also II Cor. 4:8, "perplexed, but not driven to despair," and
Ps. 23:4, "Even though I walk through the valley of the shadow
of death, I fear no evil; for Thou art with me." See p. 131,
n. 22.
8. William Gibson, *The Miracle Worker* (New York: Bantam
Pathfinder, [1960] 1964), 75.
9. *The Miracle Worker: A Play for Television* (New York: Alfred A.
Knopf, 1957), 57. This play was first presented on CBS,
"Playhouse 90," 7 February 1957.
10. Gibson, *The Miracle Worker*, 108.
11. Note how Jesus was tempted not only at the beginning of his
ministry (Luke 4:1-13), but also at Gethsemane (Luke 22:42).
12. Although Paul mentions knowing "a man in Christ," the
reference is to himself.
13. C. G. Jung, *Answer to Job* (New York: Pastoral Psychology Book
Club, 1955), 117.

14. Frank Barron in *The Study of Lives,* ed. Robert W. White (New York: Atherton Press, 1964), 247.
15. Ibid., 241.
16. Ibid.
17. Some scholars think it was epilepsy or eye trouble or malarial fever. Cf. *Interpreter's Bible* (Nashville: Abingdon Press, 1953) 10: 407, and Alexander C. Purdy, *The Interpreter's Dictionary of the Bible* 3 (1962): 689. On the "thorn" as one of Paul's "weaknesses," see Gerhard Delling, *Theological Dictionary of the New Testament* 7 (1971): 411-12, and Gustav Stählin, ibid., 1 (1964): 491-93.
18. Quoted from C. G. Jung by Roy W. Fairchild, "Pastor, Meet Dr. Jung," 10.
19. Viktor E. Frankl, *The Doctor and the Soul,* 89-90.
20. Cf. Gordon Allport's second avenue toward maturity in which humor is an important ingredient. See chap. 13, n. 17. See also Doug Adams, *Humor in the American Pulpit from George Whitefield Through Henry Ward Beecher* (North Aurora, Ill.: Sharing Co., 1976).
21. Norman Cousins, *Anatomy of an Illness,* 86.
22. Ibid., 34.
23. Ibid., 39.
24. *The Doctor and the Soul,* 228.
25. Ibid.
26. Ibid.
27. *The Study of Lives,* 247.

12. Listening / LUKE 10:38-42
A Gospel Lesson for the Ninth Sunday after Pentecost

1. This kind of incident is called a "chria" or a "pronouncement" story. The focus is on the concluding statement; that is, on the "pronouncement," and has no further reference either to Mary's or to Martha's reaction or response. See Robert C. Tannehill, ed., *Pronouncement Stories, Semeia* 20 (Chico, California: Scholars Press, 1981). On Kelber's classification "didactic" story, see chap. 3, n. 10.
2. The majority of manuscripts read "one thing is needful," but some good early manuscripts prefer "few things are needful, or only one."
3. Martin Buber, *Between Man and Man* (Boston: Beacon Press, 1955), 13-14.
4. Arthur Miller, *Death of a Salesman* in *New Voices in the American Theatre* (New York: Random House, The Modern Library, 1955), 117.

5. A plotted incident is an event or action, verbal or nonverbal, by actors referred to in a given narrative. Every plotted incident is put into causal (logical, temporal, spatial) sequence with other plotted incidents through plot devices (e.g., 10:38—"Now as they went on their way . . ."). For applications of such standard categories of literary criticism to New Testament studies, see Norman R. Petersen, *Literary Criticism for New Testament Critics* (Philadelphia: Fortress Press, 1978), 47ff. and 49ff., and Donald M. Rhoades and Donald Michie, *Mark as Story: An Introduction to the Narrative of a Gospel* (Philadelphia: Fortress Press, 1982), 73-100.

6. The Martha and Mary incident is a part of the special Lukan travel section (9:51–19:44 or 48). This section has a dual purpose: (1) God's judgment on Israel and Jerusalem, sealed with Jesus' entry into Jerusalem; and (2) the establishment of the new people of God in Jesus' presence, on Israel's soil, as a remnant. Thus Luke maintains the continuity between the old and the new people of God. Cf. Helmuth L. Egelkraut, *Jesus' Mission to Jerusalem: A Redaction Critical Study of the Travel Narrative in the Gospel of Luke 9:51 to 19:48* (Frankfurt/Bern: Lang, 1976). See also Peterson, *Literary Criticism for New Testament Critics* (above, n. 5). The travels (both in Luke 9:51ff. and in Acts) are "a major structural element in Luke's presentation of the providential leading of history . . . and in the qualification of the witnesses." The metaphor which best describes Luke's theology is "the way of the Lord." William C. Robinson, Jr., "Luke, Gospel of," *The Interpreter's Dictionary of the Bible,* Supplementary Volume (1976): 560.

7. In 9:53 the issue was of "no reception" by the Samaritans. In 10:38ff., the issue is of two different kinds of reception.

8. Mark devotes only two chapters to the journey toward Jerusalem, but Luke expands the two into eleven (chaps. 9–19) and stresses what a hard time the disciples had in facing up to change and separation.

9. Luke's Greek word *"exodus"* involves the element of joy as well as the trauma of dying to an old association (9:31, and 13:32*b*).

10. See especially 9:44-45, 13:32, and 18:32.

11. John 12:1-8 telescopes into one story the events that Luke places in two different places: 7:36-50 (in the home of Simon the Pharisee) and 10:38-42 (in the home of Martha and Mary). See chap. 7, n. 4. See also Robert C. Leslie and Margaret G. Alter, *Sustaining Intimacy: Christian Faith and Wholeness in Marriage* (Nashville: Abingdon Press, 1978), 49-51.

12. "Sitting at someone's feet" is a synonym for "listening to someone's teaching." Konrad Weiss, in *Theological Dictionary of*

the New Testament 6: 630, compares Mary's sitting at Jesus' feet with the cured demoniac's sitting at the feet of Jesus (Luke 8:35), and comments, "One can hardly say whether this attitude expresses more than grateful discipleship and a zealous readiness to learn." See also Carl Schneider, ibid., 3 (1965): 443 on "sitting as a psychological attitude" (as gesture of grief; or for "practical reasons").

13. See Peter's mother-in-law who "served them" in 4:39, and cf. the ministering women in 8:1-3, and the women in the crucifixion and resurrection stories in chaps. 23 and 24. On "Woman," her role in social and cultural structures of antiquity, see Otto J. Baab, *The Interpreter's Dictionary of the Bible* 4 (1962): 864-67; and Phyllis Trible and Robin Scroggs, ibid., Supplementary Volume (1976): 963-68.

14. For exceptions to the rule, see Bernadette Brooten, *Women Leaders in the Ancient Synagogues* (Providence: Brown University Press, 1982).

15. The Greek word is *eklegesthai,* "to choose something for oneself; to make one's choice," "to select from among many possibilities; or to decide between two possibilities," "to pick, to sift," see Gottlob Schrenk, *Theological Dictionary of the New Testament* 4 (1967): 144, 169, 172.

16. For a similar situation, see p. 39.

17. Paul Tillich, *The New Being* (New York: Scribner's, 1955), 152-60.

18. Ibid., 152 [italics ours].

13. Integrating / EPHESIANS 4:7-16
An Epistle Lesson for the Tenth Sunday after Pentecost

1. See the quotation from Ps. 68:18 (4:8) which refers to Moses. Here, and in the parenthetical comment (4:9-10), Moses is replaced by Christ.
2. C. G. Jung, "Archetypes of the Collective Unconscious," in *Psychological Reflections,* ed. Jolande Jacobi (New York: Harper Torchbooks, [1945] 1961), 217.
3. Joseph Campbell in *The Portable Jung,* ed. Joseph Campbell (New York: The Viking Press, 1971), xxi.
4. Paul Tillich, "The Lost Dimension in Religion," *The Saturday Evening Post* 230 (14 June 1958): 78.
5. James A. Michener, *Hawaii* (New York: Fawcett Crest, 1959), 1097.
6. Maya Angelou, *Singin' and Swingin' and Gettin' Merry Like Christmas* (New York: Bantam Books, [1976] 1977), 234-35.
7. Ibid., 237.

8. The one ascending ("far above all the heavens," 4:10) also descended previously ("into the lower parts of the earth," 4:9) thereby effecting that "all things" are "filled." Cf. "the measure of the stature of the fulness of Christ" (4:13). See also 1:22-23.

9. Dan Otto Via, Jr., "The Prodigal Son: A Jungian Reading," *Semeia* 9 (1977): 30 (ed. John Dominic Crossan).

10. Fritz Kunkel, *Creation Continues*, 28.

11. Arthur Miller, *After the Fall*, 30.

12. Ibid., 30-31.

13. Ibid., 163. Miller is tentative here.

14. M. Scott Peck, *The Road Less Traveled*, 17.

15. C. G. Jung, *Psychology of Religion* in *Collected Works of C. G. Jung* (Princeton, N.J.: Princeton University Press, 1973) 2: 75.

16. See above, n. 2.

17. Cf. Gordon Allport's definition of the mature person as one who develops widening interests, brings the insight of detachment (often with humor), and demonstrates integration around meaningful goals. *The Individual and His Religion* (New York: Macmillan, 1950), 53ff.

18. Probably not Paul, although the authorship is open to question. See George Johnston, "Ephesians," *The Interpreter's Dictionary of the Bible* 2 (1962): 108-9, and Nils A. Dahl, ibid., Supplementary Volume (1976): 268-69.

19. Cf. John A. Sanford, "Jesus, Paul and the Shadow," *Evil: The Shadow Side of Reality* (New York: Crossroad, 1981), 67-84.

20. Nathan Ackerman in *Critical Incidents in Psychotherapy*, ed. Stanley W. Standal and Raymond J. Corsini, 237.

14. Naming / REVELATION 21:1–22:5
An Epistle Lesson for All Saints' Day

1. All of the "sights" of the New Jerusalem, of the Bride, awaiting to be "ours" in 21:22–22:5 have their counterpart in the "promises to the conquerors" with which each of the messages to the seven churches (better: to the "angel" of the church) closes: Ephesus 2:7; Smyrna 2:11; Pergamon 2:17; Thyatira 2:26-29; Sardis 3:5; Philadelphia 3:12-13; Laodicea 3:21-22.

2. This passage is the last of the four visions which the writer "John" has on the island of Patmos: first vision, 1:9–3:22; second vision, 4:1–16:21; third vision, 17:1–21:8; fourth vision, 21:9–22:5.

3. Frank Barron, *Creativity and Psychological Health: Origins of Personal Vitality and Creative Freedom* (New York: Van Nostrand, 1963), 268-69.

4. We have already noted how Allport and Frankl belong to the same major school of personality theory. See chap. 9, n. 14.

5. Gordon W. Allport, *Becoming: Basic Considerations for a Psychology of Personality* (New Haven: Yale University Press, 1955), 12.

6. Ibid.

7. Ibid., 49.

8. From an interview recorded in a lecture-classroom demonstration in Vienna, Spring 1961. Quoted in Robert C. Leslie, *Jesus as Counselor,* 62-63.

9. Thornton Wilder, *The Skin of Our Teeth* in *Three Plays* (New York: Bantam Books, 1958), 136.

10. These thoughts, delivered in a lecture in 1959, are summarized in MacKinnon's article, "What Makes a Person Creative," *Saturday Review* 45 (10 February 1962): 17, 69.

11. See Gilles Quispel, *The Secret Book of Revelation: The Last Book of the Bible* (New York: McGraw-Hill, 1979), especially 125-26 and 129-34.

12. C. G. Jung, *Memories, Dreams, Reflections* (New York: Vintage Books, 1961), 139-40.

13. Ibid., 302.

14. M. Scott Peck, *The Road Less Traveled,* 244.

15. Ibid.

16. John Steinbeck, *East of Eden,* 240. Note, however, that for Cain the mark kept him outside, whereas in Revelation, naming gives entrance to the city.

17. The Lamb (Christ) is not the light but "God is its light, and its lamp is the Lamb" (21:23).

18. *The Skin of Our Teeth,* 135-36.

19. Frederick Buechner, *Lion Country* (New York: Atheneum Publishers, 1971), 247.

FURTHER READING SUGGESTIONS

For each chapter, three categories of reading are given:

A. liturgical
B. psychological
C. literary

CHAPTER ONE: **Waiting** / MATTHEW 1:18-25

A. Samuel Wylie and John L. McKenzie, "Advent–Christmas,"
Proclamation: Aids for Interpreting the Lessons of the Church Year (Philadelphia: Fortress Press, 1974), Series A, 1:22-28; also Paul J. Achtemeier and J. Leland Mebust, "Advent–Christmas," *Proclamation 2: Aids for Interpreting the Lessons of the Church Year* (Philadelphia: Fortress Press, 1979), Series B, 1:42.
B. Viktor E. Frankl, *Man's Search for Meaning: An Introduction to Logotherapy* (New York: Pocket Books, 1963).
Robert C. Leslie, "Pastoral Ministry During Advent," *Quarterly Review* 1 (Fall 1980): 36-43.
C. Arthur Miller, *After the Fall* (New York: Bantam World Drama, 1967).

CHAPTER TWO: **Glorifying** / LUKE 2:1-20

A. Samuel Wylie and John L. McKenzie, "Advent–Christmas," *Proclamation,* Series A, 1:28-36 (on Luke 2:1-15); also Thor Hall and James C. Price, Series B, 1 (1975): 28-35 (on Luke 2:15-20); also Reginald H. Fuller, *Proclamation 2,* Series C, 1 (1979): 28-35.
B. C. G. Jung, *Memories, Dreams, Reflections* (New York: Vintage Books, 1961).

Ann Belford Ulanov, *The Feminine in Jungian Psychology and in Christian Theology* (Evanston, Ill.: Northwestern University Press, 1971).

C. John Steinbeck, *East of Eden* (New York: Bantam, 1970).

CHAPTER THREE: **Refusing** / MARK 5:1-20

A. On Epiphany as "a time of revelation," as the season "of the revelation of Christ to the Gentiles," see "Epiphany," *Proclamation,* Series A, B, C, (1973–76) and *Proclamation 2,* Series A, B, C, (1979–82).

B. Harry Stack Sullivan, "Tensions Interpersonal and International: A Psychiatrist's View," *The Fusion of Psychiatry and Social Science* (New York: W. W. Norton & Co., 1964). Rollo May, *Love and Will* (New York: W. W. Norton & Co., 1969).

C. Theodore Isaac Rubin, *Jordi* and *Lisa and David* (New York: Ballantine Books, 1962).

CHAPTER FOUR: **Confronting** / JOHN 4:1-42

A. Charles W. F. Smith and Helmut Koester, "Lent," *Proclamation,* Series A, 3 (1974): 20-29; also Jack Dean Kingsbury and Chester Pennington, "Lent," *Proclamation 2,* Series A, 3 (1980): 35-45.

B. Virginia Satir, *Peoplemaking: So You Want to Be a Better Parent* (Palo Alto: Science and Behavior Books, 1972). J. T. Holland, "Jesus, A Model for Ministry," *Journal of Pastoral Care* 36 (December 1982): 255-64.

C. Tennessee Williams, *Cat on a Hot Tin Roof* (New York: Signet Books, 1958).

CHAPTER FIVE: **Healing** / MATTHEW 9:1-8

A. On Lent as the season when "by concentrating upon God we are pulled out of ourselves and filled with the desire to serve God," see "Lent," *Proclamation,* Series A, B, C, and *Proclamation 2,* Series A, B, C.

B. Fritz Kunkel, *Creation Continues: A Psychological Interpretation of the Gospel of Matthew* (Waco, Tex.: Word, [1946] 1973). Walter Wink, *The Bible in Human Transformation: Toward a New Paradigm for Biblical Study* (Philadelphia: Fortress Press, 1973).

C. Arthur Miller, *The Price* (New York: Bantam World Drama, 1969).

CHAPTER SIX: **Denying** / MARK 14:66-72

A. Roy A. Harrisville and Charles D. Hacket, "Holy Week," *Proclamation 2,* Series B, 4 (1981): 7-16.
B. Muriel James and Dorothy Jongeward, *Born to Win: Transactional Analysis with Gestalt Experiments* (Reading, Mass.: Addison-Wesley, 1971).
   Robert C. Leslie, *Jesus as Counselor* (Nashville: Abingdon Press Festival Book, [1965] 1982) formerly published as *Jesus and Logotherapy: The Ministry of Jesus Interpreted Through the Psychotherapy of Viktor Frankl* (Abingdon Press, 1965).
C. Ken Kesey, *One Flew Over the Cuckoo's Nest* (New York: Viking Compass, 1964).

CHAPTER SEVEN: **Washing** / JOHN 13:1-15

A. Krister Stendahl, "Holy Week," *Proclamation,* Series A, 4:38-47; also Richard L. Jeske and Browne Barr, "Holy Week," *Proclamation 2,* Series A, 4 (1980): 42-53.
B. Robert C. Leslie, PSR Occasional Paper 1 (January 1974), Pacific School of Religion, Berkeley, Calif. 94709.
   Roy W. Fairchild, "Pastor, Meet Dr. Jung," *Pacific Theological Review* 7 (Winter 1975): 4-10, San Francisco Theological Seminary, San Anselmo, Calif. 94960.
C. Thornton Wilder, *The Eighth Day* (New York: Harper & Row, 1967).

CHAPTER EIGHT: **Preparing** / MARK 16:1-8

A. Charles Rice and J. Louis Martyn, "Easter," *Proclamation,* Series B, 5 (1975): 1-7; also George W. MacRae and Charles P. Price, "Easter," *Proclamation 2,* Series B, 5:7-13.
B. Edgar Jackson, *You and Your Grief* (New York: Channel Press, 1964).
   M. Scott Peck, *The Road Less Traveled: A New Psychology of Love, Traditional Values and Spiritual Growth* (New York: Simon & Schuster Touchstone, 1978).
C. Alan Paton, *Too Late the Phalarope* (New York: Scribner's, 1953).

CHAPTER NINE: **Rejoicing** / I PETER 1:3-9

A. John H. Snow and Victor P. Furnish, "Easter," *Proclamation,* Series A, 5 (1975): 14-20; also Bruce Vawter and William J. Carl III, "Easter," *Proclamation 2,* Series A, 5: 23-28.

B. Robert C. Leslie, "Counseling Across Cultures," United Ministries in Higher Education Monograph Number 5 (June 1979). Available from Educational Ministries, American Baptist Church, Valley Forge, Penn. 19481.
   Karl Barth, *Deliverance to the Captives* (New York: Harper & Brothers, 1961).
C. Arther Miller, *The Crucible* (New York: Bantam World Drama, 1966).

CHAPTER TEN: **Enabling** / ACTS 2:1-21

A. David Randolph and Jack Kingsbury, "Pentecost 1," *Proclamation,* Series B, 6 (1975): 1-8; also Howard Clark Kee and Peter J. Gomes, "Pentecost 1," *Proclamation 2,* Series C, 6 (1980): 7-12.
B. Elisabeth Kübler-Ross, *Living with Death and Dying* (New York: Macmillan, 1981).
   James Ashbrook, "The Name of the Game: Babel—Legion—Pentecost," *Journal of Pastoral Care* 36 (June 1982): 118-24.
C. Mary Ellen Chase, *Windswept* (New York: Macmillan, 1941).

CHAPTER ELEVEN: **Laughing** / II CORINTHIANS 11:21*b*–12:10

A. David Randolph and Jack Kingsbury, "Pentecost 1," *Proclamation,* Series B, 6 (1975): 35–43 (on II Cor. 12:7-10), also Leander E. Keck and Francis W. Hobbie, "Pentecost 1," *Proclamation 2,* Series B, 6 (1982): 47-53.
B. Frank Barron, *Creativity and Psychological Health: Origins of Personal Vitality and Creative Freedom* (New York: Van Nostrand, 1963).
   Norman Cousins, *Anatomy of an Illness as Perceived by the Patient: Reflections on Healing and Regeneration* (New York: W. W. Norton & Co., 1979).
C. William Gibson, *The Miracle Worker: A Play for Television* (New York: Alfred A. Knopf, 1957).

CHAPTER TWELVE: **Listening** / LUKE 10:38-42

A. Ronald E. Sleeth and John R. Donahue, "Pentecost 1," *Proclamation,* Series C, 6 (1974): 53-58; also Howard Clark Kee and Peter J. Gomes, "Pentecost 1," *Proclamation 2,* Series C, (1980): 57-62.
B. Elisabeth Moltmann-Wendel, "Mary Magdalene: An Example of Patriarchal Distortion of History," and "The Domesticated

Martha," cassettes from Pacific School of Religion Pastoral Conferences, 17–18 February 1982, Pacific School of Religion, Berkeley, Calif. 94709.

Robert C. Leslie and Margaret G. Alter, *Sustaining Intimacy: Christian Faith and Wholeness in Marriage* (Nashville: Abingdon Press, 1978), 44-64.

C. Arthur Miller, *Death of a Salesman* (New York: The Viking Press, [1949] 1958).

CHAPTER THIRTEEN: **Integrating** / EPHESIANS 4:7-16

A. Eduard Riegert and Richard H. Hiers, "Pentecost 2," *Proclamation,* Series B, 7 (1975): 1-6; also A. Y. Collins and Charles Rice, "Pentecost 2," *Proclamation 2,* Series B, 7 (1982): 8-12.

B. Gordon Allport, *The Individual and His Religion* (New York: Macmillan, 1950).
Paul Tillich, "The Lost Dimension in Religion," *Saturday Evening Post* 230 (14 June 1958): 58ff.

C. Maya Angelou, *Singin' and Swingin' and Gettin' Merry Like Christmas* (New York: Bantam Books, 1977).

CHAPTER FOURTEEN: **Naming** / REVELATION 21:1–22:5

A. Philip Pfatteicher, "The Lesser Festivals 2," *Proclamation,* Series D, 2 (1975): 41-45; also Lorenz Nieting, "Lesser Festivals," *Proclamation 2,* Series D, 4 (1981): 26-31.

B. Gordon Allport, *Becoming: Basic Considerations for a Psychology of Personality* (New Haven: Yale University Press, 1955).
Ann Belford Ulanov, *Receiving Woman: Studies in the Psychology and Theology of the Feminine* (Philadelphia: The Westminster Press, 1981).

C. Thornton Wilder, *The Skin of Our Teeth* in *Three Plays* (New York: Bantam Books, 1958).

READINGS IN THE DIALOGUE BETWEEN PSYCHOLOGY AND BIBLICAL STUDY

Note: The readings are in addition to the references cited in the footnotes and in the Further Reading Suggestions for each of the chapters.

On Psychology and General Biblical Study

Capps, Donald. *Biblical Approaches to Pastoral Counseling*. Philadelphia: The Westminster Press, 1981. See especially "The Bible's Role in Pastoral Counseling," a historical survey of writings since the late 1930s, 17-46.

Diel, P. *La Symbolisme dans la théologie. Sa signification psychologique.* Petite Bibl. Payot. Paris, 1975.

Homans, Peter. "Psychology and Hermeneutics: An Exploration of Basic Issues and Resources." *Journal of Religion* 55 (1975): 327-47.

Oden, Thomas C. "Revelation and Psychotherapy." Nr. I, *Continuum* 2:2 (1964): 239-64; Nr. III, *Continuum* 3:1 (1965): 91-95.

Oglesby, William B., Jr. *Biblical Themes for Pastoral Care*. Nashville: Abingdon Press, 1980.

Outler, Albert. *Psychotherapy and the Christian Message*. New York: Harper & Brothers, 1954.

Roberts, David. *Psychotherapy and a Christian View of Man*. New York: Charles Scribner's Sons, 1959.

Rollins, Wayne G., *Jung and the Bible*. Atlanta: John Knox Press, 1983.

Stern, E. Mark, and Marino, Bert G. *Psychotheology*. Paramus, N.J.: Newman Press, 1970.

Vergote, A. "Psychanalyse et interprétation biblique," edited by H. Cazelles and A. Feuillet. *Supplément au Dictionnaire de la Bible* 9 (Paris, 1979): 252-60 (with bibliography).

Wink, Walter. "On Wrestling with God: Using Psychological Insights in Biblical Study." *Religion in Life* 47 (1978): 136-47.
Wise, C. A. *Pastoral Psychotherapy: Theory and Practice.* New York: Jason Aronson, 1980.

On Psychology and the Study of Jesus and the Gospels

Bonnell, John Sutherland. *Do You Want to Be Healed?* New York: Harper & Row, 1968.
Fowler, Robert M. "Using Literary Criticism of the Gospels." *Christian Century* 99 (26 May 1982): 626-29.
Greeley, Andrew M. "Pop Psychology and the Gospel." *Theology Today* 33 (1976): 224-31.
Moltmann-Wendel, Elisabeth. *The Women Around Jesus: Reflections on Authentic Personhood.* New York: Crossroad, 1982.
Powell, L. Mack. "Parallel Thoughts in the Practice of Psychotherapy and the New Testament." *The Journal of Pastoral Care* 15 (Summer 1961) 86-94.
Sanford, John A. *The Kingdom Within: A Study of the Inner Meaning of Jesus' Sayings.* Philadelphia: Lippincott, 1970.
Schweitzer, Albert. *The Psychiatric Study of Jesus.* Boston: Beacon Press, (1948) 1958.
Sladeck, P. "Kehret um! (Mark 1:15): Die Umkehrforderung des Evangeliums im Lichte einer christlichen Tiefenpsychologie." *Ordens-Korrespondenz* 15 (Cologne, 1974): 173-84.
Tenzler, J. "Tiefenpsychologie und Wunderfrage." *Münchener Theologische Zeitschrift* 25 (1974): 118-37.
Ward, Colleen A., and Michael H. Beaubrun. "The Psychodynamics of Demon Possession." *Journal of the Scientific Study of Religion* 19 (June 1980): 201-7.

On Psychology and the Study of Paul and the Epistles

Bishop, J. G. "Psychological Insights in St. Paul's Mysticism." *Theology* 78 (1975): 318-24.
Moore, Robert L. "Pauline Theology and the Return of the Repressed: Depth Psychology and Early Christian Thought." *Zygon* 13 (1978): 158-68.
Rubenstein, Richard. *My Brother Paul.* New York: Harper & Row, 1972.
Sanford, John A. "Jesus, Paul and Depth Psychology." *Religious Education* 68 (1973): 673-89.
Scroggs, Robin. *Paul for a New Day.* Philadelphia: Fortress Press, 1977.

INDEX